PESTICI

PESTICIDE ALERT

ALERT

A GUIDE TO PESTICIDES IN FRUITS AND VEGETABLES

**LAWRIE MOTT
and KAREN SNYDER**

*Natural Resources
Defense Council* NRDC

Sierra Club Books   San Francisco

The Sierra Club, founded in 1892 by John Muir, has devoted itself to the study and protection of the earth's scenic and ecological resources—mountains, wetlands, woodlands, wild shores and rivers, deserts and plains. The publishing program of the Sierra Club offers books to the public as a nonprofit educational service in the hope that they may enlarge the public's understanding of the Club's basic concerns. The point of view expressed in each book, however, does not necessarily represent that of the Club. The Sierra Club has some sixty chapters coast to coast, in Canada, Hawaii, and Alaska. For information about how you may participate in its programs to preserve wilderness and the quality of life, please address inquiries to Sierra Club, 730 Polk Street, San Francisco, CA 94109.

The Natural Resources Defense Council is a nonprofit membership organization dedicated to protecting natural resources and improving the quality of the human environment. With offices in New York City, Washington, D.C. and San Francisco, NRDC combines legal action, scientific research, and citizen education in its environmental protection program. For more information, write NRDC, 122 East 42nd Street, New York, NY 10168.

Library of Congress Cataloging-in-Publication Data

Mott, Lawrie.
   Pesticide alert.

   Bibliography: p.
   Includes index.
   1. Pesticide residues in food—United States.
I. Snyder, Karen, 1964–   . II. Title.
TX571.P4M67   1988   363.1'92'0973   87–42965
ISBN 0-87156-726-1 (pbk.)
ISBN 0-87156-728-8

Cover design by Paul Bacon
Book design by Abigail Johnston
Production by Susan Ristow

Printed in the United States of America

10 9 8 7 6 5 4 3 2

Acknowledgments

The research for this book was funded by the Beldon Fund, the Columbia Foundation, the Wallace Alexander Gerbode Foundation, the Richard and Rhoda Goldman Fund, the Legacy Fund of the Institute for Regional Education, the Charles Stewart Mott Foundation, the Public Welfare Foundation, the San Francisco Foundation, the L.J. Skaggs and Mary C. Skaggs Foundation and the Strong Foundation for Environmental Values. In addition, support was received from the general membership of the Natural Resources Defense Council.

Preface

Food is one of the fundamental necessities of life. Yet, a growing body of evidence, documented in *Pesticide Alert,* indicates that our food supply is being contaminated with pesticides—dangerous, life-threatening chemicals.

Just how real is this danger and what can we do about it? Up to now, most of the scientific data regarding pesticide contamination of food has been buried in research reports and government documents, virtually inaccessible to the layperson. Now, for the first time, NRDC pesticide experts, Lawrie Mott and Karen Snyder, have brought together this documented evidence and made it comprehensible to the public.

It is easy to become cynical about pesticides in food. The solutions appear to be far beyond the grasp of an individual, but there is little trust that government regulatory agencies will protect the public health. Can we afford to throw up our hands and leave this problem to others to solve?

As Chair of the Subcommittee on Health and the Environment, I am fully aware of the health and environmental dangers we face from pesticides. I am confident about the future, though, because I believe consumers have the power to force change. Americans have responded to information regarding threats to our health in significant ways: we have cut down on smoking, reduced fats from our diets, and begun to exercise more. In the process, we've used the power of the purse to change the way that American industries make and sell their products.

The strength of the American consumer has already been felt on the issue of pesticides in food. Some conventional supermarkets are now selling food grown without pesticides; several manufacturers have announced that they would not accept food treated with a dangerous pesticide; and farmers are switching to agricultural methods that use less, or no, pesticides.

The demand for a safer, more wholesome food supply is also being felt in the halls of Congress and the corridors of those agencies charged with protecting public health, including the Environmental Protection Agency and the Food and Drug Administration. The changes in government regulation of pesticides which are now under discussion are being driven by the expressions of concern that you convey to us. In the battle for safer food, *Pesticide Alert* is a welcome new weapon to arm consumers for effective citizen action.

Congressman Henry A. Waxman
Chairman, Subcommittee on Health
and the Environment
U.S. House of Representatives

Contents

1 Pesticide residues in food

When you go to the supermarket, if you are like most Americans, you try to choose foods that are healthy. Instinctively you steer your shopping cart towards the produce section. The average American now eats 26 pounds more fresh fruits and vegetables per year than ten years ago. The typical produce section currently stocks over five times the number of items displayed a decade ago.[1] The increased availability and variety of fresh fruits and vegetables is, in part, due to the extensive use of chemical fertilizers and pesticides. Yet residues of these agricultural chemicals can remain in our food. The fruits and vegetables in your supermarket may contain invisible hazards to your health in the form of residues of pesticides.

All of us are exposed to pesticides on a regular basis. The food we eat, particularly the fresh fruits and vegetables, contains pesticide residues. In the summer of 1985, nearly 1,000 people in several Western states and Canada were poisoned by residues of the pesticide Temik in watermelons. Within two to twelve hours after eating the contaminated watermelons, people experienced nausea, vomiting, blurred vision, muscle weakness and other symptoms. Fortunately, no one died, though some of the victims were gravely ill. Reports included grand mal seizures, cardiac irregularities, a number of hospitalizations, and at least two stillbirths following maternal illness.[2]

During 1986, the public grew increasingly concerned over the use of the plant growth regulator Alar on apples. Primarily used to make the harvest easier and the apples redder, Alar leaves residues in both apple juice and apple sauce. The outcry led many food manufacturers and supermarket chains to announce they would not accept Alar-treated apples. Also in 1986, approximately 140 dairy herds in Arkansas, Oklahoma, and Missouri were quarantined due to contamination by the banned pesticide heptachlor. Dairy products in eight states were subject to recall. Some milk contained heptachlor in amounts as much as seven times the acceptable level.[3] Those responsible for the contamination were sentenced to prison terms.[4] Several years earlier, it was the news media rather than the regulatory agencies that alerted the public to high levels of the pesticide EDB in muffin and cake mixes, cereals, and citrus. Given these incidents, it is not surprising that three out of four consumers consider pesticides in food a serious hazard, according to a 1987 food industry survey.[5]

The National Academy of Sciences issued, in 1987, a report on pesticides in the food supply. On the basis of data in the study, the potential risks posed by cancer-causing pesticides in our food are over one million additional cancer cases in the United States population over our lifetimes.[6] Although some have argued that this theoretical calculation is excessively high, the number was based on the presence of fewer than 30 carcinogenic pesticides in our food supply (many more pesticides applied to food are carcinogens) and does not consider potential exposure to carcinogenic pesticides in drinking water.

The repetition of the Temik, EDB, Alar, and other stories suggests that the government programs designed to protect us from pesticide residues may be inherently flawed. These events also demonstrate the need for information on a series of fundamental issues concerning pesticide residues in food. As it now stands, you have no way of knowing if your food contains dangerous residues or whether the amount of residue you are eating is hazardous. Not only is government testing of food for residues spotty and inadequate, not only are some levels of pesticides allowed in food being challenged by leading scientists as too high, but no state or federal government agency really attempts to answer your most basic questions about pesticide residues in food—questions such as what pesticides are found in your food, what level of residue is safe and who should make these decisions.

This Guide will provide information on pesticides in food. For each of the most commonly-consumed fresh fruits and vegetables, this Guide identifies the pesticides that are found most frequently as residues, the potential health effects associated with these chemicals, and whether the residues can be washed off. This Guide does not cover other parts of our food supply, such as canned fruits and vegetables, meat, milk or grains that contain pesticides because information on the presence of pesticides in these foods is limited.

In the short run, this information can help you make more informed choices. There are some steps you can take to reduce your exposure to pesticides in food, such as buying organically grown produce and avoiding fruits and vegetables imported from nations with weak pesticide regulatory programs.

In the long run, we need to reduce agriculture's reliance on chemicals substantially. Methods to produce food with little or no pesticides have existed for many years. Some examples of reductions in pesticide use through integrated pest management and other methods are provided on page 46. But more research needs to be done to expand these techniques, and the nation's food producers must be encouraged to switch to these methods. You can participate directly in resolving the problems posed by pesticide residues in food. If consumers begin to look for and demand safer food, farmers will be forced to reduce their use of pesticides and make changes that will significantly benefit our health and protect the environment.

By choosing foods with fewer chemicals, you can send a direct message to the food industry that will speed the transition away from hazardous pesticides in agriculture. Even food companies can now take steps to reduce the levels of pesticides in their products. In a March 13, 1986 letter to growers, the H.J. Heinz Company announced that food treated with any of 13 pesticides EPA is reviewing as a potential health hazard will not be used to manufacture baby food. You can also make the government do a better job of protecting our food supply and regulating these chemicals.

The ideal solution to the current problems posed by pesticide residues in our food has five different components:

1. Organic food should be made available in regular supermarkets. You should have the right to choose between different types of produce.
2. All produce should be labelled to identify where the food was grown and what pesticide residues it contains. This information would allow you to make more informed choices when purchasing produce.
3. The Environmental Protection Agency (EPA) should regulate pesticide use more stringently, and set tougher limits on pesticide levels in food so that the residues occurring are safe.
4. The Food and Drug Administration (FDA) should improve and expand its monitoring for pesticides in food in order to prevent consumers from eating food containing dangerous residues.
5. Agricultural production methods should be modified to reduce reliance on chemical pesticides. Food should be grown without chemicals used to improve the cosmetic appearance of our fruits and vegetables. Sustainable agriculture—farming that renews and regenerates the land—would be better for our health and the environment.

These changes will not come overnight, though some are already occurring. Several California supermarkets have adopted an independent program to identify pesticides in the produce sold in their stores. Organic produce is available in certain Boston food stores. Some national chain stores have said they would offer organic produce if requested by customers. By our efforts individually and together, we can ensure that these goals become reality. This Guide will tell you steps to take that will benefit your health and protect the environment from the dangers of pesticides.

How are pesticides used?

Each year approximately 2.6 billion pounds of pesticides are used in the United States.[7] Pesticides are applied in countless ways, not just on food crops. They are sprayed on forests, lakes, city parks, lawns, and playing fields, and in hospitals, schools, offices, and homes. They are also contained in a huge variety of products from shampoos to shelf paper, mattresses to shower curtains. As a consequence, pesticides may be found wherever we live and work, in the air we breathe, in the water we drink, and in the food we eat. A former director of the federal government's program to regulate pesticides called these chemicals the number one environmental risk, because all Americans are exposed to them.[8]

By definition, pesticides are toxic chemicals—toxic to insects, weeds, fungi, and other unwanted pests. Most are potentially harmful to humans and can cause cancer, birth defects, changes in genetic material that may be inherited by the next generation (genetic mutations), and nerve damage, among other debilitating or lethal effects. Many more of these chemicals have not been thoroughly tested to identify their health effects.

Pesticides applied in agriculture—the production of food, animal feed, and fiber, such as cotton—account for 60 percent of all U.S. pesticide uses other than disinfectants and wood preservatives.[9] Pesticides are designed to control or destroy undesirable pests. Insecticides control insects; herbicides control weeds; fungicides control fungi such as mold and mildew; and rodenticides control rodents. Some of these chemicals are applied to control pests that reduce crop yields or to protect the nutritional value of our food; others are used for cosmetic purposes to enhance the appearance of fresh food.

How does agricultural use of pesticides affect humans?

As a result of massive agricultural applications of pesticides, our food, drinking water, and the world around us now contain pesticide residues; they are literally everywhere—in the United States and throughout the world. In fact, though all these chemicals have been banned from agricultural use, nearly all Americans have residues of the pesticides DDT, chlordane, heptachlor, aldrin, and dieldrin in their bodies.[10] Ground water is the source of drinking water for 95 percent of rural Americans and 50 percent of all Americans. Yet, according to a 1987 Environmental Protection Agency (EPA) report, at least 20 pesticides, some of which cause cancer and other harmful effects, have been found in ground water in at least 24 states.[11] In California alone, 57 different pesticides have been detected in the ground water.[12] The banned pesticide DBCP remains in 2,499 drinking water wells in California's San Joaquin Valley— 1,473 of these contaminated wells are not considered suitable for drinking water or bathing because the DBCP levels exceed the state health department's action level.[13] As more states conduct ground water sampling programs for pesticides, more pesticides are expected to be found. Surface water supplies have also been found to contain pesticides. For example, the herbicide alachlor, or Lasso, has contaminated both ground and surface water in the Midwest, primarily as a result of use on corn and soybeans. Meanwhile, the federal government provides financial assistance to cotton and soybean farmers because enormous surpluses of these crops exist in the United States.

The extent of contamination of our food is unknown. The Federal Food and Drug Administration (FDA) monitors our food supply to detect pesticide residues. Between 1982 and 1985, FDA detected pesticide residues in 48 percent of the most frequently consumed fresh fruits and vegetables. This figure probably understates the presence of pesticides in food because about half of the pesticides applied to food cannot be detected by FDA's routine laboratory methods, and FDA samples less than one percent of our food.[14]

The cumulative effect of widespread, chronic low-level exposure to pesticides is only partially understood. Some of the only examples now available involve farmers and field workers. A National Cancer Institute study found that farmers exposed to herbicides had a six times greater risk than nonfarmers of contracting one type of cancer.[15] Other studies have shown similar results, with farmers exposed to pesticides having an increased risk of developing cancer.[16] See "Work Is Hazardous" on page 114. Researchers at the University of Southern California uncovered startling results in a 1987 study sponsored by the National Cancer Institute. Children living in homes where household and garden pesticides were used had as much as a sevenfold greater chance of developing childhood leukemia.[17]

Another frightening consequence of the long-term and increasing use of pesticides is that the pest species farmers try to control are becoming resistant to these chemicals. For example, the number of insects resistant to insecticides nearly doubled between 1970 and 1980.[18] Resistance among weeds and fungi has also risen sharply in the last two decades. In order to combat this problem, greater amounts of pesticides must be applied to control the pest, which in turn can increase the pest's resistance to the chemical. For example, since the 1940s pesticide use has increased tenfold, but crop losses to insects have doubled.[19]

Pesticides can also have detrimental effects on the environment. The widespread use of chlorinated insecticides, particularly DDT, significantly reduced bird populations, affecting bald eagles, ospreys, peregrine falcons, and brown pelicans. DDT is very persistent and highly mobile in the environment. Animals in the Antarctic and from areas never sprayed have been found to contain DDT or its metabolites.[20] Though most of the organochlorines are no longer used in the United States, continuing use in other nations has serious environmental consequences. Other types of pesticides now applied in the United States have adverse effects on the environment. See "Environmental Effects" on page 58.

How concerned should consumers be about pesticides in food?

A February 1987 EPA report, entitled *Unfinished Business,* ranked pesticides in food as one of the nation's most serious health and environmental problems.[21] Many pesticides widely used on food are known to cause, or are suspected of causing, cancer. To date, EPA has identified 55 cancer-causing pesticides that may leave residues in food.[22] Other pesticides can cause birth defects or miscarriages. Some pesticides can produce changes in the genetic material, or genetic mutations, that can be passed to the next generation. Other pesticides can cause sterility or impaired fertility.

Under today's scientific practices, predictions of the potential adverse health effects of chemicals on humans are based on laboratory testing in animals. Unfortunately, the overwhelming majority of pesticides used today have not been sufficiently tested for their health hazards. The National Academy of Sciences estimated, by looking at a selected number of chemicals, that data to conduct a thorough assessment of health effects were available for only ten percent of the ingredients in pesticide products used today.[23]

A 1982 Congressional report estimated that between 82 percent and 85 percent of pesticides registered for use had not been adequately tested for their ability to cause cancer; the figure was 60 percent to 70 percent for birth defects, and 90 percent to 93 percent for genetic mutations.[24] This situation has occurred because the majority of pesticides now available were licensed for use before EPA established requirements for health effects testing.

In 1972, Congress directed EPA to reevaluate all these older chemicals (approximately 600) by the modern testing regimens. Through reregistration, EPA would fill the gaps in required toxicology tests. Roughly 400 pesticides are registered for use on food, and 390 of these are older chemicals that are undergoing reregistration review.[25] By 1986, however, EPA still had not completed a final safety reassessment for any of these chemicals. To make matters worse, scientists are uncovering new types of adverse health effects caused by chemicals. For example, a few pesticides have been found to damage components of the immune system—the body's defense network to protect against infections, cancer, allergies, and autoimmune diseases.[26] Yet testing for toxicity to the immune system is not part of the routine safety evaluation for chemicals. In short, pesticides are being widely used with virtually no knowledge of their potential long-term effects on human health and the human population is unknowingly serving as the test subject.

The lack of health effects data on pesticides means that EPA is regulating pesticides out of ignorance, rather than knowledge. This poses particularly serious consequences for EPA's regulation of pesticides in food. Pesticides may only be applied to a food crop after EPA has established a maximum safe level, or tolerance, for pesticide residues allowed in the food. However, EPA's tolerances may permit unsafe levels of pesticides for five reasons:

1. EPA established tolerances without necessary health and safety data.
2. EPA relied on outdated assumptions about what constitutes an average diet, such as assuming we eat no more than 7.5 ounces per year of avocado, artichokes, melon, mushrooms, eggplants or nectarines, when setting tolerance levels.
3. Tolerances are rarely revised when new scientific data about the risks of a pesticide are received by EPA.
4. Ingredients in pesticides that may leave hazardous residues in food, such as the so-called, "inert" ingredients, are not considered in tolerance setting. (See "Inert But Not Benign" on page 62.)
5. EPA's tolerances allow carcinogenic pesticide residues to occur in food, even though no "safe" level of exposure to a carcinogen may exist.

The EPA is not solely responsible for the flaws in the federal government program to protect our food supply. The FDA monitors food to ensure that residue levels do not exceed EPA's tolerances. Food containing pesticide residues in excess of the applicable tolerance violates the food safety law and FDA is required to seize this food in order to prevent human consumption. However, FDA is not always capable of determining which foods have illegal pesticide residues. For instance, FDA's routine laboratory methods can detect fewer than half the pesticides that may leave residues in food. Some of the pesticides used extensively on food that cannot be regularly identified include alachlor, benomyl, daminozide, and the EBDCs. Furthermore, FDA's enforcement against food with residues in excess of tolerance is ineffective; according to a 1986 General Accounting Office report, for 60 percent of the illegal pesticide residue cases identified, FDA did not prevent the sale or the ultimate consumption of the food.[27] For more details on the EPA and FDA programs, see "Federal Regulation of Pesticides: A Record of Neglect" on page 135.

An illustration of EPA's inadequate regulation of pesticides in food

To understand the potential risks associated with pesticide residues in food, consider the case of the pesticide captan. This chemical is widely used in fruits and vegetables, and is a common residue in food. Although the levels of captan usually found in food are below EPA's tolerances, even these residues may not be safe for four reasons. First, EPA has called this chemical a probable human carcinogen; therefore, any level of exposure may cause cancer. Second, the majority of captan tolerances were set before EPA knew the chemical caused cancer. Third, the tolerances do not cover one of the compound's breakdown products that may also be a carcinogen. Fourth, EPA's determinations of what levels of captan in food should be acceptable do not consider exposure to captan through nonfood sources such as paints, mattresses, shower curtains, and shampoos. Although EPA began a special review of this chemical in 1980 because of concerns about its hazards, by 1987 the Agency still had taken no steps to restrict the use of the chemical or protect the public.

How this Guide was developed

This Guide identifies some of the pesticide residues that are found most frequently in 26 kinds of fresh fruits and vegetables. The results are summarized in the chart on the following pages. The data were obtained from the federal government's and California Department of Food and Agriculture's pesticide residue monitoring programs. Because both the state and federal governments' laboratory tests cannot detect about half the pesticides used on food, many agricultural chemicals present in our food may not have been detected. California's results were included because the state program focuses on California grown foods, and California supplies the nation with 51 percent of its fresh vegetables and a significant proportion of its fresh fruit.[28] The FDA does not extensively sample California food, in order to avoid duplication of the state's program. The combined results from both monitoring systems provide a more complete picture of pesticide residues in food nationwide.

For the purposes of this Guide, all pesticide residues detected—regardless of the amount—were identified in each type of produce. Most of the residues occurred in amounts below EPA's tolerances. However, even residues below tolerance may not be safe because EPA's tolerance setting system is seriously flawed. Many EPA tolerances were established without adequate health and safety data, or by relying on inappropriate assumptions about our diet. Therefore, the tolerances may have been set too high. In addition, the Delaney clause of the federal food safety law prohibits the use of cancer-causing food additives *in any amount*. However, the same law permits EPA to allow the presence of carcinogenic pesticides in food. There is no evidence to support this double standard because carcinogenic pesticide residues in food are no less dangerous to human health than other carcinogenic substances added to our food.

GUIDE SUMMARY
Pesticides most commonly detected by commodity

Commodity	Pesticides	Can residues be reduced by washing?
Apples	Diphenylamine	Unknown
	Captan*	Yes
	Endosulfan	Unknown
	Phosmet	Yes
	Azinphos-methyl	Yes
Bananas	Diazinon	Unknown
	Thiabendazole	Yes
	Carbaryl	Yes
Bell Peppers	Methamidophos	No
	Chlorpyrifos	Unknown
	Dimethoate	Unknown
	Acephate	No
	Endosulfan	Unknown
Broccoli	DCPA	Unknown
	Methamidophos	No
	Dimethoate	Unknown
	Demeton	No
	Parathion	Unknown
Cabbage	Methamidophos	No
	Dimethoate	Unknown
	Fenvalerate	Unknown
	Permethrin	Yes
	BHC	Unknown
Cantaloupes	Methamidophos	No
	Endosulfan	Unknown
	Chlorothalonil	Yes
	Dimethoate	Unknown
	Methyl Parathion	Unknown

Pesticides in bold type are especially hazardous.

Commodity	Pesticides	Can residues be reduced by washing?
Carrots	**DDT**	Yes
	Trifluralin	No
	Parathion	Unknown
	Diazinon	Unknown
	Dieldrin	Unknown
Cauliflower	Methamidophos	No
	Dimethoate	Unknown
	Chlorothalonil	Yes
	Diazinon	Unknown
	Endosulfan	Unknown
Celery	Dicloran	Yes
	Chlorothalonil	Yes
	Endosulfan	Unknown
	Acephate	No
	Methamidophos	No
Cherries	**Parathion**	Unknown
	Malathion	Yes
	Captan	Yes
	Dicloran	Yes
	Diazinon	Unknown
Corn	**Sulfallate**	Unknown
	Carbaryl	Yes
	Chlorpyrifos	Unknown
	Dieldrin	Unknown
	Lindane	Unknown
Cucumbers	Methamidophos	No
	Endosulfan	Unknown
	Dieldrin	Unknown
	Chlorpyrifos	Unknown
	Dimethoate	Unknown
Grapefruit	Thiabendazole	Yes
	Ethion	Yes
	Methidathion	Unknown
	Chlorobenzilate	Yes
	Carbaryl	Yes

Commodity	Pesticides	Can residues be reduced by washing?
Grapes	Captan	Yes
	Dimethoate	Unknown
	Dicloran	Yes
	Carbaryl	Yes
	Iprodione	Unknown
Green Beans	Dimethoate	Unknown
	Methamidophos	No
	Endosulfan	Unknown
	Acephate	No
	Chlorothalonil	Yes
Lettuce	Mevinphos	No
	Endosulfan	Unknown
	Permethrin	Yes
	Dimethoate	Unknown
	Methomyl	No
Onions	DCPA	Unknown
	DDT	Yes
	Ethion	Yes
	Diazinon	Unknown
	Malathion	Yes
Oranges	Methidathion	Unknown
	Chlorpyrifos	Unknown
	Ethion	Yes
	Parathion	Unknown
	Carbaryl	Yes
Peaches	Dicloran	Yes
	Captan	Yes
	Parathion	Unknown
	Carbaryl	Yes
	Endosulfan	Unknown
Pears	Azinphos-methyl	Yes
	Cyhexatin	Unknown
	Phosmet	Yes
	Endosulfan	Unknown
	Ethion	Yes

Commodity	Pesticides	Can residues be reduced by washing?
Potatoes	**DDT**	Yes
	Chlorpropham	No
	Dieldrin	Unknown
	Aldicarb	No
	Chlordane	Unknown
Spinach	Endosulfan	Unknown
	DDT	Yes
	Methomyl	No
	Methamidophos	No
	Dimethoate	Unknown
Strawberries	**Captan**	Yes
	Vinclozolin	Unknown
	Endosulfan	Unknown
	Methamidophos	No
	Methyl Parathion	Unknown
Sweet Potatoes	Dicloran	Yes
	Phosmet	Yes
	DDT	Yes
	Dieldrin	Unknown
	BHC	Unknown
Tomatoes	Methamidophos	No
	Chlorpyrifos	Unknown
	Chlorothalonil	Yes
	Permethrin	Yes
	Dimethoate	Unknown
Watermelon	Methamidophos	No
	Chlorothalonil	Yes
	Dimethoate	Unknown
	Carbaryl	Yes
	Captan	Yes

Another reason for identifying all pesticide residues is that with certain health hazards, especially cancer, any amount of exposure may be dangerous. This is in contrast to the general belief that the toxic effects of a chemical will not occur until a minimum threshold level of exposure is reached. As the exposure level increases—especially over the threshold—the toxicity increases. Most experts believe that no threshold exists for delineating safe and unsafe exposure to carcinogens. Former EPA Administrator William Ruckelshaus agreed with this position by announcing "the Agency is assuming a no-threshold approach for regulating carcinogens."[29] This means that any amount of carcinogenic pesticide residues in our food poses a risk. Until scientists fully comprehend how cancer occurs, and how we can prevent it, we must reduce our exposure to carcinogens.

Exposure to any level of pesticide residues is also cause for concern because the possibility of synergism exists. Synergism is when the simultaneous exposure to more than one chemical produces a greater toxic effect than the straight sum of the chemicals' individual toxicities. Each fruit or vegetable may contain more than one kind of pesticide, and an entire meal of different foods may expose us to several different pesticides.

Some pesticide residues occur in food in small amounts and may or may not be cause for immediate health concern. However, the public has a right to know what chemicals are occurring in food regardless of the amount.

What pesticides do our fresh fruits and vegetables contain?

To obtain a picture of the pesticides that occur in the foods most commonly eaten, NRDC analyzed representative federal and state pesticide monitoring data. From 1982 to 1985, FDA analyzed 19,415 samples of the 26 types of fruits and vegetables nationwide. Forty-eight percent contained detectable residues. In the same period, the California Department of Food and

Agriculture (CDFA) analyzed 17,237 produce samples. Pesticide residues were detected in 14 percent of the samples. These numbers most likely understate the amount of pesticides in food because the laboratory tests cannot detect all the chemicals applied to our food. The discrepancy between FDA and CDFA's results is probably due to FDA's ability to detect a greater number of chemicals in lower amounts and the greater number of imported samples analyzed by FDA.

Over 110 different pesticides were detected in all these foods between 1982 and 1985. Of the 25 pesticides detected most frequently, nine have been identified by EPA to cause cancer (captan, chlorothalonil, permethrin, acephate, DDT, parathion, dieldrin, methomyl, and folpet). Two of these carcinogens, DDT and dieldrin, were banned from use in the United States in 1972 and 1974 respectively due to their carcinogenicity and environmental persistence. DDT and dieldrin residues occurring in food result either from the continued use of these chemicals in foreign nations exporting food to this country, or from contamination by trace levels of the chemicals persisting in the U.S. environment. Table 1 identifies the pesticides most commonly detected in fresh fruit and vegetables.

Certain fruits and vegetables are likely to contain pesticides more frequently than others. For some fruits and vegetables, including strawberries and peaches, high standards about the cosmetic appearance of the food result in greater pesticide use. Foods with edible portions grown directly in contact with soil, such as celery, carrots and potatoes, may act as sponges and absorb chemical residues from the soil. Other fruits and vegetables have naturally occurring barriers to some pesticide residues, including thick skins on bananas, husks on corn, and wrapper leaves on cauliflower. In Table 2, foods (both domestic and imported) are listed in order of the presence of pesticide residues.

The FDA program specifically identified samples of imported food that were analyzed. Between 1982 and 1985, approximately 40 percent of all FDA's sampling of these fruits and vegetables was of imported foods. Of the imported foods analyzed,

TABLE 1
Pesticides most commonly detected in fresh fruits and vegetables

Pesticide	Use & Initial date of registration	Potential hazards
Acephate	insecticide (1972)	cancer, mutagenicity, reproductive toxicity
Aldicarb	insecticide (1970)	severely toxic at small doses
Azinphos-methyl	insecticide (1956)	data under review
BHC	insecticide (1963)	cancer, reproductive toxicity
Captan	fungicide (1951)	cancer, mutagenicity
Carbaryl	insecticide (1958)	kidney effects, mutagenicity
Chlordane	insecticide (1948)	cancer, birth defects, reproductive toxicity, mutagenicity
Chlorobenzilate	insecticide (1953)	cancer, reproductive toxicity
Chlorothalonil	fungicide (1966)	cancer, chronic effects, mutagenicity
Chlorpropham	herbicide (1962)	mutagenicity
Chlorpyrifos	insecticide (1965)	data gaps
Cyhexatin	insecticide (1972)	birth defects, chronic effects
DCPA	herbicide (1958)	data gaps
DDT	insecticide (1945)	cancer, reproductive toxicity, liver effects
Demeton	insecticide (1955)	birth defects, mutagencity

Pesticide	Use & initial date of registration	Potential hazards
Diazinon	insecticide (1952)	neurobehavioral effects
Dicloran	fungicide (1961)	data gaps
Dieldrin	insecticide (1949)	cancer, birth defects, reproductive toxicity
Dimethoate	insecticide (1963)	cancer, birth defects, reproductive toxicity, mutagenicity
Diphenylamine	plant growth regulator/ insecticide (1962)	kidney and blood effects
Endosulfan	insecticide (early 1960s)	chronic effects
Ethion	insecticide (1972)	data under review
Fenvalerate	insecticide (1979)	cancer
Iprodione	fungicide (1980)	chronic effects, mutagenicity
Lindane	insecticide (1950)	cancer, chronic effects
Malathion	insecticide (1950s)	reproductive toxicity
Methamidophos	insecticide (1972)	data under review
Methidathion	insecticide (1972)	cancer
Methomyl	insecticide (1963)	chronic effects, mutagenicity
Methyl Parathion	insecticide (1954)	cancer, chronic effects, mutagenicity
Mevinphos	insecticide (1958)	mutagenicity
Parathion	insecticide (1948)	cancer, mutagenicity
Permethrin	insecticide (1978)	cancer, reproductive toxicity

Pesticide	Use & initial date of registration	Potential hazards
Phosmet	insecticide (1966)	cancer, mutagenicity
Sulfallate	herbicide (1973)	cancer, mutagenicity
Thiabendazole	fungicide (1968)	inadequate information available
Trifluralin	herbicide (1963)	cancer, chronic effects
Vinclozolin	fungicide (1981)	mutagenicity

pesticide residues were detected in 64 percent; in comparison, 38 percent of the domestic foods were found to have pesticide residues (see Table 3).

For all but six of the individual food commodities, imported foods contained more pesticide residues than the domestically grown foods (see Table 4). In some cases, the imported foods had pesticide residues over twice as frequently. For example, 23 percent of the domestically grown tomatoes contained pesticides, whereas 70 percent of the imported tomatoes had residues. Thirty percent of the domestic cucumbers had residues, while 80 percent of the imported cucumbers contained residues.

What consumers can do

Below are some steps you can take to limit your exposure to pesticides in fresh food. In the long term, the best way to minimize the presence of pesticides in food is by reducing the widespread use of pesticides in agriculture. Consumers can accelerate this transition in agriculture through their power in the marketplace. By demanding food without pesticide residues, or at least with less, consumers will deliver a clear message to our food producers and provide an incentive for farmers to decrease their use of pesticides. Specific advice on removing pesticides from food is difficult to offer because data on this issue are generally scarce.

TABLE 2
Frequency of residue detection in foods

Commodity	Percent of domestic and imported samples with pesticide residues
Strawberries	63%
Peaches	55%
Celery	53%
Cherries	52%
Cucumbers	51%
Bell Peppers	49%
Tomatoes	45%
Sweet Potatoes	37%
Cantaloupes	34%
Grapes	34%
Lettuce	32%
Apples	29%
Spinach	29%
Carrots	28%
Green Beans	27%
Pears	22%
Grapefruit	22%
Potatoes	22%
Oranges	22%
Cabbage	20%
Broccoli	13%
Onions	10%
Cauliflower	5%
Watermelon	4%
Bananas	1%
Corn	1%

TABLE 3
FDA's imported and domestic food samples

Sample type	Total number of samples	Total number with residues	Percent with residues
Domestic	11,729 (60%)	4,450	38%
Imported	7,686 (40%)	4,922	64%
Total	19,415	9,372	48%

1. Wash all produce.
In order to decrease exposure to pesticides in food, consumers should wash all fresh fruits and vegetables in water. This will remove *some but not all* pesticide residues on the surface of produce. A mild solution of dish washing soap and water may help remove additional surface pesticide residues.

2. Peel produce when appropriate.
Peeling fruit and vegetable skins will also help to avoid some pesticide residues. Peeling the skin from produce will completely remove pesticide residues contained as surface residues. Residues contained inside the fruit or vegetable will not be eliminated by peeling. Unfortunately, through peeling you may lose some of the valuable nutrients contained in fresh food.

3. Grow your own food.
You may consider growing some of your own food. With a small sunny area you can plant vegetables in a garden, or even planter boxes. For instance, it is relatively easy to grow lettuce, tomatoes or zucchini. Since you are growing the food, you can choose whether you want to apply chemical pesticides, and if you do use pesticides, you can select the safest ones possible.

4. Buy organically grown fruits and vegetables.
Consumers should consider buying organically grown fruits and vegetables. Alternative methods to chemical pest control have been available for many years and their use is increasing

TABLE 4
Comparison of pesticide contamination in domestic and imported foods

Commodity	Percent of FDA's imported samples with residues	Percent of FDA's domestic samples with residues
Apples	53%	48%
Bananas	2%	0%
Bell Peppers	81%	30%
Broccoli	33%	14%
Cabbage	53%	20%
Cantaloupes	78%	11%
Carrots	58%	46%
Cauliflower	16%	2%
Celery	75%	72%
Cherries	65%	62%
Corn	5%	1%
Cucumbers	80%	30%
Grapefruit	52%	63%
Grapes	44%	28%
Green Beans	46%	27%
Lettuce	57%	52%
Onions	18%	28%
Oranges	49%	36%
Peaches	58%	53%
Pears	35%	45%
Potatoes	24%	39%
Spinach	23%	42%
Strawberries	86%	70%
Sweet Potatoes	11%	30%
Tomatoes	70%	23%
Watermelon	25%	2%

in certain crops. Yet these methods have been neglected because chemicals seemed so effective and their ecological and health dangers were not well understood. Most organically grown food is produced entirely without chemicals during the growing, harvesting, shipping or storage stages. Some states, such as California, Oregon, Maine, Massachusetts, Minnesota, Nebraska, Montana and Washington have both strict definitions of what can be called organic food and certification schemes to verify that food sold as organic is organic.

Alternative pest control techniques will not be expanded and used until consumers decide that the current dependence on chemicals is unacceptable. By seeking and buying organically grown food, shoppers are sending an undeniable message about their desire to avoid pesticides—and providing an incentive for farmers to produce organically grown food. Farmers may be more willing to change their agricultural methods if they believe consumers will support their efforts. Further, if growers perceived a larger demand for organic food, they would switch their pest control techniques, and increased amounts of organic food would be available.

The first place to start is your local supermarket. Consumers can request that their regular supermarket sell organically grown produce. All 125 Safeway stores in the United Kingdom, for example, stock organic produce.[30] In 1987, Raley's, a chain of 50 supermarkets in northern California and Nevada, began a program to offer organically grown fruits and vegetables in all its stores. Several major American supermarket chains have said they would offer organic food if the demand existed. Most stores could locate a steady supply of organic food. Some organizations involved with sustainable agriculture have published directories of wholesale suppliers and distributors of organic food. (Three of these directories, *Healthy Harvest, The Organic Network,* and *Organic Wholesalers Directory and Yearbook,* are listed in the "Further References" section.) You may want to suggest that your supermarket get such a directory, or directly contact the organization that compiled the directory for a recommendation about the best sources of organic food. The group that certifies organic food in your state, such as the California Certified Organic Farmers, could also identify good suppliers and wholesalers of organic food.

Other sources of organic food include natural food stores and cooperatives. Check your local phone book. Also ask at farmers' markets and U-Pick farms where organic food is available. Your nearest organization for certification of organic growers may also be able to steer you to a source of organically grown fruits and vegetables. (See the Organic Crop Improvement Association described in the "Sources of Additional Information" section.)

5. Buy domestically grown produce and buy produce in season.

Imported produce generally contains more pesticide residues than domestically grown fruits and vegetables. Produce imported from other nations may contain residues of pesticides that are banned from use in the United States. Also, many food exporting nations in the developing world lack stringent pesticide regulations. You should request that your supermarket label the origin of the produce. Was it grown in the United States or in a foreign country? Produce shipping containers frequently identify the source of the food so it should be easy for supermarkets to provide you with this information.

6. Beware of perfect looking produce.

Consumers should also think twice about pursuing the perfect peach. Nature is not flawless. Many chemical pesticides are used to enhance the cosmetic appearance of fruits and vegetables. Farmers claim they use pesticides because of consumer insistence on perfect looking produce. A brown spot on the surface of an apple does not decrease the nutritional value of the fruit nor does it affect the taste. We must recognize that the price of perfect looking fruits and vegetables often is more pesticide residues.

7. Meet with your supermarket manager.

Consumers should schedule appointments with their supermarket managers, or with representatives from the consumer affairs department of the supermarket, to discuss their concerns about the health threats of pesticides. Supermarkets are usually responsive to their customers. Let the produce manager and the supermarket company know that you are concerned about pesticide residues in food and would like to know what chemicals are present in the food you buy there. Although the store may not be able to answer your questions right away, if enough customers ask, the employees will find time to get the information. Explore, with a supermarket representative, various options for obtaining more information on what pesticide residues may be in the food the store sells. Perhaps the store could post information on pesticides that have been used on the food. Ask the produce manager if he or she knows the original source of the produce and what pesticides have been used on the produce and might be present as residues. The federal food safety law requires that any pesticides used on food after harvest must be labelled on the shipping container. These pesticides could easily be identified for you, if produce shippers have complied with the law. If the manager does not know about the chemicals used on food before harvest, suggest that he or she ask the produce wholesaler or even the grower directly. The agricultural extension agent in your county may also know about what pesticides are typically applied.

Tell store officials that industry leaders are moving toward safe food. Bread and Circus, a chain of four Boston food stores, does a successful business selling "safe food." [31] In addition, Grand Union supermarkets, an East Coast chain of more than 300 stores, are marketing "natural beef," and test-marketing "natural chicken." [32]

8. Write your federal and state government officials.
For better or worse, in the near future we must rely primarily on the government to protect us from pesticides in food. However, consumers can make the government do a better job. You can write to FDA and EPA to express your concerns as a consumer about pesticide residues in food and the inadequacies in their programs to regulate these substances. Private

citizens can make the difference in government decisions to ban dangerous chemicals. You can also contact your state health and agricultural officials to find out about state programs on pesticide residues in food.

9. Write to your congressional representatives.

All citizens should write their senators and representatives to inform them about the health threats posed by pesticides. In particular, you can urge that they support stricter controls on pesticide use, increased research on alternatives to chemical pest control, and creation of incentives for farmers to employ the alternative methods. Elected representatives need to hear from their constituents, and they ought to be responsive to their constituents' concerns. You might suggest that they put pressure on the federal and state government agencies to do a better job of protecting consumers from pesticides in food. You can also correspond with your elected officials at the state and local level.

2 How to use this Guide

The pages in this section identify the five pesticides most frequently detected for each fruit or vegetable, according to the federal and California monitoring programs. This Guide does not list all the different chemicals that were found in each food. Furthermore, some pesticides are being used on our food that cannot be identified by the routine laboratory tests. The government programs generally analyze food samples as whole commodities and without washing the foods. For example, bananas and oranges are analyzed whole, *e.g.,* with peels. However, caps are removed from strawberries, roots, stems, and outer sheaches are removed from onions, and the tops of carrots are discarded.

For each pesticide, what is currently known about the chemical's health effects is summarized. Adverse effects such as cancer or genetic mutations are presented. The risk of any toxicity increases with the level of exposure and the amounts of pesticide residues found in food were generally low (in the parts per million to parts per billion range). However, some chemicals are cause for concern regardless of how small the amount present in our food. These chemicals are printed in bold type. For some chemicals, incomplete information is available about potential long-term health effects because the pesticides have not been adequately tested. The EPA requires the following toxicology studies to predict the chronic health hazards of pesticides:

Chronic toxicity tests—2 species
Oncogenicity (cancer) tests—2 species
Teratogenicity (birth defects) tests—2 species
Reproductive toxicity test—1 species
Mutagenicity tests—3 studies

(The chronic toxicity and oncogenicity tests are sometimes combined and conducted on the same set of animals.) Gaps in the required chronic toxicity data are identified on the following pages.

Information on whether residues can be removed with water washing is presented for each pesticide. Two factors determine whether water will remove residues of a pesticide from food: (1) are the residues limited to the surface of the food (*e.g.,* not distributed inside the food), and (2) can the pesticide be dissolved in water.

Unfortunately, most pesticides cannot be removed with water. Some pesticides retained only on the surface of produce can be partially or completely removed with water washing or completely removed with peeling. However, many pesticides are formulated specifically so they will not be soluble in water because farmers do not want them to wash off plants in the field when it rains. Furthermore, much of our produce is waxed after harvesting in order to preserve its appearance. This process, in effect, seals the pesticide residues in the food. In fact, some pesticides are even combined with the waxes. For instance, waxes applied to citrus and tomatoes may contain fungicides. (See "Waxed Produce" on page 126.) Finally, systemic residues—those which are distributed throughout the food—simply cannot be avoided.

APPLES

Every year, Americans on average eat 22 pounds of apples per person. Nearly one-third of the apples sampled were found to contain residues of one or more pesticides. Forty-three different pesticides were detected in apples. However, the routine laboratory method used by the federal government can detect only half of the more than 110 pesticides that can be applied to apples. The EPA has registered more pesticides for use on apples than any other fruit or vegetable listed in this Guide. Here are the five pesticides detected most frequently (in order of decreasing occurrence) in fresh apples:

Pesticide	Health effects
Diphenylamine *DPA*	Some evidence of adverse kidney and blood effects in animal studies. According to EPA, has not been sufficiently tested for long-term health effects.
Captan *Merpan, Orthocide*	Probable human carcinogen. Some evidence of mutagenic effects in laboratory test systems. EPA initiated Special Review in 1980 due to carcinogenicity, mutagenic effects, and presence of residues in food.
Endosulfan *Thiodan*	Some evidence of adverse chronic effects including liver and kidney damage and testicular atrophy in test animals. No observed mutagenic effects in laboratory test systems.
Phosmet *Imidan*	Possible human carcinogen. Some evidence of mutagenic effects in laboratory test systems and humans (pesticide factory workers). No observed birth defects or reproductive toxicity in animal studies.
Azinphos-methyl *Guthion*	EPA is reviewing studies submitted to fill previous data gaps for carcinogenicity, birth defects, reproductive toxicity, and mutagenic effects.

Can residue be reduced by washing?	Residue reduction
UNKNOWN	Residues remain primarily in the peel. DPA does not readily dissolve in water; therefore, plain water washing may not reduce residues, but peeling may help.
YES	Residues remain primarily on the produce surface. However, the metabolite THPI, a suspected carcinogen, may be systemic. Washing, cooking, or heat processing will reduce residues.
UNKNOWN	Residues remain primarily on the produce surface; however, endosulfan metabolites may be systemic. Peeling, cooking, or heat processing may reduce residues slightly. No information on removal with water.
YES	Residues remain primarily on the produce surface. Washing or cooking will reduce residues.
YES	Residues remain primarily on the produce surface. Washing, cooking, or heat processing will reduce residues.

An apple a day won't keep the doctor away

Daminozide, or Alar, is a plant growth regulator reportedly applied to approximately 38% of the fresh apples grown in the United States. Apples treated with daminozide ripen more slowly, are less likely to drop from the trees before harvest and have deeper, more uniform color. The main types of apples treated with daminozide are MacIntosh, Red and Golden Delicious, Jonathan, and Stayman. When daminozide-treated apples are made into apple juice or apple sauce, the breakdown product UDMH is formed. Five separate studies completed between 1973 and 1984 have shown daminozide and UDMH to be carcinogens. The EPA proposed to cancel all food uses of daminozide in the fall of 1985, but retracted this position in early 1986 and allowed use to continue essentially without restriction. In the results of FDA's food monitoring, residues of daminozide are not found frequently because the federal government's routine laboratory methods cannot detect daminozide or UDMH. However, according to special tests that EPA required Uniroyal—the pesticide manufacturer, to conduct, daminozide and UDMH contamination is widespread. Daminozide and UDMH were detected in 87% and 71%, respectively, of the samples of fresh apples, apple juice and sauce, peanuts and peanut butter, cherry filling and Concord grape juice that were analyzed. Many manufacturers of apple juice and apple sauce have announced they will no longer accept daminozide-treated apples for use in their products. Some supermarkets have also stated that daminozide-treated apples will not be sold in their stores. The EPA plans to review daminozide again in 1989.

As "American" as apple pie?

Imports of apples to the United States increased by 90 percent from 1982 to 1986. In fact, nearly 300 million pounds of apples were imported in 1986. Apples are imported from as many as 40 different countries, yet only 12% of the apples analyzed by FDA from 1982 to 1986 were imported. Further, over half of these apple samples had residues.

BANANAS

E very year, Americans on average eat 11 pounds of bananas per person. Only one percent of the sampled bananas was found to contain pesticide residues. The EPA has registered more than 30 different pesticides for use on bananas, but FDA's routine laboratory method can detect only half of these chemicals. Thick banana peels may prevent pesticides from being absorbed into the fruit. In addition, there is some evidence that green bananas (the typical banana is harvested and shipped while still green) are immune to many of the diseases that plague ripe fruits. Ninety-two percent of the bananas analyzed by FDA were imported. Here are the three pesticides that were detected in fresh bananas:

Pesticide	Health effects
Diazinon *Spectrocide, Sarolex*	Some evidence of adverse neurobehavioral effects in the developing offspring of test animals in one study. No observed carcinogenicity or reproductive toxicity in animal studies.
Thiabendazole *TBZ, Mertect*	No observed carcinogenicity or birth defects in test animals.
Carbaryl *Sevin*	Some evidence of adverse kidney effects in humans, and mutagenic effects in laboratory test systems. No observed carcinogenicity or reproductive toxicity in animal studies.

Can residue be reduced by washing?	Residue reduction
UNKNOWN	Residues remain primarily on the produce surface. No information on removal with water.
YES	Residues are primarily found in the peel. Peeling or washing will reduce residues.
YES	Residues remain primarily on the produce surface. Washing or peeling will reduce residues.

Banana imports

Over 17 billion pounds of bananas were imported into the United States from 1983–1985. During the same time period, FDA analyzed a total of 139 samples of imported bananas. Bananas were imported into the United States from 50 different countries over this three-year period and from 19 countries in each of the three years. Bananas from 10 of the 50 nations were not sampled in any of the three years.

BELL PEPPERS

Half of all sampled fresh bell peppers were found to contain residues of one or more pesticides. Thirty-nine different pesticides were detected in bell peppers. The EPA has registered more than 70 different pesticides for use on bell peppers, but FDA's routine laboratory method can only detect 60% of these chemicals. Over one-third of the samples had methamidophos residues, and 15% had chlorpyrifos and dimethoate residues. Here are the five pesticides detected most frequently (in order of decreasing occurrence) in fresh bell peppers:

Pesticide	Health effects
Methamidophos *Monitor*	No observed birth defects in one animal study. EPA is reviewing studies submitted to fill previous data gaps for carcinogenicity, birth defects, reproductive toxicity and mutagenic effects.
Chlorpyrifos *Dursban*	No observed carcinogenicity, birth defects or mutagenic effects in available studies. According to EPA, has not been sufficiently tested for chronic toxicity, carcinogenicity, or mutagenic effects.
Dimethoate *Cygon, Rogon*	Some evidence of carcinogenicity, birth defects, reproductive toxicity and mutagenic effects in laboratory studies.
Acephate *Orthene*	Possible human carcinogen. Some evidence of mutagenic effects in laboratory test systems, and reproductive toxicity in one animal study.
Endosulfan *Thiodan*	Some evidence of adverse chronic effects including liver and kidney damage and testicular atrophy in test animals. No observed mutagenic effects in laboratory test systems.

Can residue be reduced by washing?	Residue reduction
NO	Residues are systemic and probably cannot be removed with washing.
UNKNOWN	Residues remain primarily on the produce surface. No information on removal with water. Dried fruits showed higher levels of residues than on fresh fruits because of the concentration effect of dehydration.
UNKNOWN	Residues are systemic. However, washing, peeling, cooking, or heat processing reduced residues in various studies.
NO	Residues are systemic and probably cannot be removed with washing. Cooking or canning may reduce residues.
UNKNOWN	Residues remain primarily on the produce surface; however, endosulfan metabolites may be systemic. Peeling, cooking, or heat processing may reduce residues slightly. No information on removal with water.

Imported bell peppers

Over 600 million pounds of all kinds of peppers were imported into the United States from 1983–1985. Peppers were imported into the United States from 53 different countries during this three-year period and from 21 nations in each of the three years. Peppers from 11 of the 53 countries were not sampled in any of the three years.

Over 2000 bell pepper samples were analyzed from 1982–1985; they were the fourth most frequently sampled commodity in this Guide. Imports accounted for 77% of FDA's samples, and 80% of these imported bell peppers contained pesticide residues. Imported bell peppers contained more pesticide residues than any other imported vegetable analyzed by FDA.

BROCCOLI

Thirteen percent of the fresh broccoli sampled were found to contain residues of one or more pesticides. Twenty-three different pesticides were detected in the broccoli analyzed. The EPA has registered more than 50 different pesticides for use on broccoli, and FDA's routine laboratory method can detect 70% of these chemicals. Here are the five pesticides detected most frequently (in order of decreasing occurrence) in fresh broccoli:

Pesticide	Health effects
DCPA *Dacthal,* *Chlorthal-* *dimethyl*	No observed birth defects in laboratory studies. According to EPA, has not been sufficiently tested for carcinogenicity or mutagenic effects.
Methamidophos *Monitor*	No observed birth defects in one animal study. EPA is reviewing studies submitted to fill previous data gaps for carcinogenicity, birth defects, reproductive toxicity and mutagenic effects.
Dimethoate *Cygon, Rogon*	Some evidence of carcinogenicity, birth defects, reproductive toxicity and mutagenic effects in laboratory studies.
Demeton *Systox*	Some evidence of birth defects and mutagenic effects in laboratory studies. According to EPA, has not been sufficiently tested for carcinogenicity, birth defects, reproductive toxicity, or mutagenic effects.
Parathion *Phoskil*	Possible human carcinogen. Some evidence of mutagenic effects in laboratory studies. No observed reproductive toxicity or birth defects in animal studies.

Can residue be reduced by washing?	Residue reduction
UNKNOWN	Some evidence that residues are systemic. For a preemergence herbicide, the relatively frequent findings of residues indicate a fair degree of persistence. No information on removal with water.
NO	Residues are systemic and probably cannot be removed with washing.
UNKNOWN	Residues are systemic. However, washing, peeling, cooking, or heat processing reduced residues in various studies.
NO	Residues are systemic and probably cannot be removed with washing.
UNKNOWN	Residues remain primarily on the produce surface. Washing, peeling, cooking, or heat processing may reduce residues slightly.

Reducing pesticide use: The IPM story

Methods to significantly reduce pesticide use on specific crops have been demonstrated, but not widely applied. Integrated pest management, or IPM, relies on pest monitoring to pinpoint when pesticide applications will have the maximum effect. For example, pesticides are sprayed only after the pest population reaches a level that will damage the crop or when the pest is most vulnerable to the effects of the pesticide. Other approaches include planting crop varieties that resist pest damage, and using biological controls that assault pests with their natural enemies, including predators, parasites, and pathogens.

Employment of these techniques has already resulted in some remarkable decreases in pesticide use. For example in Texas, the use of insecticides on cotton dropped by 88% between 1966 and 1974 through a system of integrated pest management. IPM programs in grain sorghum, cotton and peanuts reduced insecticide use by 41%, 75%, and 81% respectively. Sweet corn growers in Connecticut cut insecticide consumption by up to 50%, with an average reduction of 25%, using IPM. Growers employing similar techniques in California pear orchards report that pesticide use is down by an average of 30%.

Other studies have identified significant potential reductions in chemical use that have not yet been achieved. A 1979 report by the Office of Technology Assessment of the U.S. Congress concluded that a national commitment to IPM could reduce pesticide applications by up to 75%. Another study projected a 70% to 80% reduction at no cost in crop yields, if IPM was employed nationwide in cotton, citrus, deciduous fruits, soybeans, and alfalfa.

CABBAGE

E very year, Americans eat on average nearly five pounds of cabbage per person. Twenty percent of the cabbage sampled was found to contain residues of one or more pesticides. Thirty-six different pesticides were detected in cabbage. The EPA has registered more than 60 different pesticides for use on cabbage, and FDA's routine laboratory method can detect nearly 70% of these chemicals. Here are the five pesticides detected most frequently (in order of decreasing occurrence) in fresh cabbage:

Pesticide	Health effects
Methamidophos *Monitor*	No observed birth defects in one animal study. EPA is reviewing studies submitted to fill previous data gaps for carcinogenicity, birth defects, reproductive toxicity and mutagenic effects.
Dimethoate *Cygon, Rogon*	Some evidence of carcinogenicity, birth defects, reproductive toxicity and mutagenic effects in laboratory studies.
Fenvalerate *Pydrin, Belmark*	Some evidence of carcinogenicity in the only available studies. No observed birth defects, reproductive toxicity, or mutagenic effects in laboratory studies.
Permethrin *Ambush, Pounce*	Possible human carcinogen. Some evidence of reproductive toxicity in one animal study. No observed birth defects or mutagenic effects in laboratory studies.
BHC *HCH, 666, Hexachlor*	Causes cancer in test animals. Some evidence of male reproductive toxicity in test animals. EPA cancelled all uses in U.S. in 1978 due to carcinogenicity. Residues persist in the environment.

Can residue be reduced by washing?	Residue reduction
NO	Residues are systemic and probably cannot be removed with washing. Residues remain primarily in the outer leaves of lettuce, so stripping these tough layers in cabbage may reduce residues.
UNKNOWN	Residues are systemic. However, washing, peeling, cooking, or heat processing reduced residues in various studies.
UNKNOWN	Residues remain primarily on the produce surface. Fenvalerate does not readily dissolve in water; therefore, plain water washing may not reduce residues.
YES	Residues remain primarily on the produce surface. Washing with detergent will reduce residues; plain water may not.
UNKNOWN	Residues remain primarily on the produce surface. No information on removal with water.

Pesticide resistance or mutant insects

The example of pesticide resistance many of us have personally experienced is the ubiquitous, and virtually indestructible, cockroach. Over 440 species of insects have now developed genetic resistance to the chemicals designed to kill them. The National Academy of Sciences reports that almost every major insect in farmers' fields today is resistant to more than one category of pesticide. Twenty-three species have become resistant to every kind of pesticide available. Once an insect becomes resistant, pesticides need to be sprayed even more frequently to combat the pest. The costs of pesticide resistance have not been quantified, but one estimate puts the resulting additional insecticide applications in the United States at $130 million annually. (Total direct costs of pesticide control measures were $2.8 billion.) Probably three times that amount is at stake if resistance in plant pathogens (fungi), weeds, root worms, and rodents is considered.

Resistance occurs when pesticides kill nearly every individual in a pest population, but some individuals survive due to a unique combination of genes. The survivors bounce back rapidly because the pesticide has also killed their natural enemies. The pesticide-resistant genes are then found in a much larger portion of the population. Repeated applications of stronger doses of pesticides only exacerbate the problem of resistance. Susceptible insects are weeded out, and resistant survivors thrive and pass their genetic traits to their thousands of offspring. Before long, an entire population carries the gene for pesticide resistance. Possible solutions to this include integrated pest management and biological pest control.

CANTALOUPES

One-third of the cantaloupes sampled were found to contain residues of one or more pesticides. Thirty different pesticides were detected in cantaloupes. The EPA has registered more than 70 pesticides for use on cantaloupes, and FDA's routine laboratory method can detect only 55% of these chemicals. Methamidophos and endosulfan residues were detected in 15% of all samples. Here are the five pesticides detected most frequently (in order of decreasing occurrence) in fresh cantaloupes:

Pesticide	Health effects
Methamidophos *Monitor*	No observed birth defects in one animal study. EPA is reviewing studies submitted to fill previous data gaps for carcinogenicity, birth defects, reproductive toxicity and mutagenic effects.
Endosulfan *Thiodan*	Some evidence of adverse chronic effects including liver and kidney damage and testicular atrophy in test animals. No observed mutagenic effects in laboratory test systems.
Chlorothalonil *Bravo*	Probable human carcinogen. Some evidence of chronic health effects including kidney, thyroid, stomach and liver changes, and mutagenic effects in laboratory studies. No observed birth defects in animal studies. Hexachlorobenzene contaminant is a probable human carcinogen and is found in food.
Dimethoate *Cygon, Rogon*	Some evidence of carcinogenicity, birth defects, reproductive toxicity and mutagenic effects in laboratory studies.
Methyl Parathion *Folidol M, Metacide*	Some evidence of carcinogenicity and adverse chronic health effects including blood changes in animal studies. Some evidence of mutagenic effects in laboratory test systems. According to EPA, has not been sufficiently tested for carcinogenicity or birth defects.

Can residue be reduced by washing?	Residue reduction
NO	Residues are systemic and probably cannot be removed with washing.
UNKNOWN	Residues remain primarily on the produce surface; however, endosulfan metabolites may be systemic. Peeling may reduce residues slightly. No information on removal with water.
YES	Residues remain primarily on the produce surface; however, chlorothalonil metabolites may be systemic. Washing reduces residues.
UNKNOWN	Residues are systemic. However, washing and peeling reduced residues in various studies.
UNKNOWN	Residues remain primarily on the produce surface, but some evidence that residues can be absorbed. No information on removal with water.

Imported cantaloupes

Imports of cantaloupes to the United States increased by 73% from 1982 to 1986. Over 300 million pounds of cantaloupes were imported in 1986. Imported cantaloupes accounted for 60% of FDA's samples and nearly 80% of these contained residues. By comparison, only 11% of FDA's domestic samples had detectable pesticide residues.

There were at least six shipments of Mexican cantaloupes with illegal pesticide residues detected by FDA's Los Angeles laboratory in 1986. Three of these shipments were exported to other countries with less protective restrictions, and two shipments were sold in the United States because FDA allows some shipments of perishable food to be sold before the results of the sample analysis are known.

CARROTS

Every year, Americans on average eat eight pounds of carrots per person. One-quarter of the carrots sampled were found to contain residues of one or more pesticides. Thirty different pesticides were detected in carrots. The EPA has registered almost 50 different chemicals for use on carrots, but FDA's routine laboratory method can only detect 50% of these chemicals. DDT was found in 17% of the domestic carrot samples analyzed by FDA. This high frequency results from DDT's persistence in the environment, particularly residues in the soil. Here are the five pesticides detected most frequently (in order of decreasing occurrence) in fresh carrots:

Pesticide	Health effects
DDT	Probable human carcinogen. Some evidence of reproductive toxicity, and adverse liver effects in animal studies. EPA cancelled all uses in the U.S. in 1972 due to carcinogenicity, bioaccumulation, and other chronic effects.
Trifluralin *Treflan*	Possible human carcinogen. Some evidence of adverse health effects including kidney changes in test animals. No observed birth defects, reproductive toxicity or mutagenic effects in laboratory studies.
Parathion *Phoskil*	Possible human carcinogen. Some evidence of mutagenic effects in laboratory studies. No observed reproductive toxicity or birth defects in animal studies.
Diazinon *Spectrocide, Sarolex*	Some evidence of adverse neurobehavioral effects in the developing offspring of test animals in one study. No observed carcinogenicity or reproductive toxicity in animal studies.
Dieldrin	Probable human carcinogen. Causes birth defects and reproductive toxicity in animal studies. Low levels cause adverse effects on learning capabilities in monkeys. EPA cancelled all uses in the U.S. in 1974 due to carcinogenicity, bioaccumulation, and other chronic effects.

Can residue be reduced by washing?	Residue reduction
YES	Residues remain primarily on the produce surface, although residues may be absorbed into the peel. Washing and peeling reduce residues in root crops, but cooking won't reduce residues once they have been absorbed into the plant tissue.
NO	Residues are systemic and probably cannot be removed with washing, particularly in root crops. Peeling may reduce residues in carrots.
UNKNOWN	Residues remain primarily on the produce surface. Washing, peeling, cooking, or heat processing may reduce residues slightly.
UNKNOWN	Residues remain primarily on the produce surface. Cooking or heat processing may reduce residues. No information on removal with water.
UNKNOWN	Residues remain primarily on the produce surface, although there is some evidence that residues are systemic in root crops. No information on removal with water. Peeling or cooking may reduce residues.

Environmental effects

Many of us remember the story of DDT. First introduced as a pesticide after World War II, DDT was considered a modern miracle. Then the chemical's environmental persistence and tendency to accumulate in living organisms was discovered. Public outcry over residues of DDT in fish and its threat to bird reproduction due to thinning of eggshells contributed to EPA's decision to ban its further use in 1972. Eventually nearly all the environmentally-persistent organochlorines, or DDT's chemical cousins—dieldrin, aldrin, heptachlor, endrin, and toxaphene—were cancelled.

Other pesticides still in use continue to threaten the environment. Birds have fallen victim to organophosphate use on grasslands; in one incident, 700 Atlantic Brant geese were killed after feeding on a Long Island golf course that was treated with diazinon. The entire New York population of Atlantic Brant geese was estimated at 2,500 in 1984. Diazinon has been confirmed or implicated in approximately 60 separate bird-kills involving 23 species of birds, including migratory and nonmigratory waterfowl, song birds, shore birds, and others. Chlorpyrifos, another organophosphate, is highly toxic to fish, birds, and other wildlife, and has the potential to affect over 100 endangered species according to EPA. Finally, endosulfan has been linked to several fish-kills in California.

A 1986 report written for EPA generally condemned the Agency for failing to investigate pesticide poisonings of endangered species, including the Bald Eagle, Gray Bat, Brown Pelican, and the California Condor. The study also criticized EPA for taking insufficient actions to address risks to other endangered species previously identified by the United States Fish and Wildlife Service. The EPA now estimates that approximately 250 of the 450 species on the endangered species list are potentially jeopardized by pesticide use in 47 states.

CAULI-FLOWER

Only five percent of the fresh cauliflower samples were found to contain residues of one or more pesticides. The protective outer leaves on cauliflower plants may prevent pesticide residues from being absorbed into the edible portion. Seventeen different pesticides were detected on cauliflower. The EPA has registered nearly 60 different chemicals for use on cauliflower, and FDA's routine laboratory method can detect almost 70% of these chemicals. Here are the five pesticides detected most frequently (in order of descending occurrence) in fresh cauliflower:

Pesticide	Health effects
Methamidophos *Monitor*	No observed birth defects in one animal study. EPA is reviewing studies submitted to fill previous data gaps for carcinogenicity, birth defects, reproductive toxicity and mutagenic effects.
Dimethoate *Cygon, Rogon*	Some evidence of carcinogenicity, birth defects, reproductive toxicity and mutagenic effects in laboratory studies.
Chlorothalonil *Bravo*	Probable human carcinogen. Some evidence of chronic health effects including kidney, thyroid, stomach and liver changes, and mutagenic effects in laboratory studies. No observed birth defects in animal studies. Hexachlorobenzene contaminant is a probable human carcinogen and found in food.
Diazinon *Spectrocide, Sarolex*	Some evidence of adverse neurobehavioral effects in the developing offspring of test animals in one study. No observed carcinogenicity or reproductive toxicity in animal studies.
Endosulfan *Thiodan*	Some evidence of adverse chronic effects including liver and kidney damage and testicular atrophy in test animals. No observed mutagenic effects in laboratory test systems.

Can residue be reduced by washing?	Residue reduction
NO	Residues are systemic and probably cannot be removed with washing.
UNKNOWN	Residues are systemic. However, washing, peeling, cooking, or heat processing reduced residues in various studies.
YES	Residues remain primarily on the produce surface; however, chlorothalonil metabolites may be systemic. Washing or cooking reduces residues.
UNKNOWN	Residues remain primarily on the produce surface. Cooking or heat processing may reduce residues. No information on removal with water.
UNKNOWN	Residues remain primarily on the produce surface; however, endosulfan metabolites may be systemic. Peeling, cooking, or heat processing may reduce residues slightly. No information on removal with water.

Inert but not benign

Pesticide products contain both an active ingredient used to control the pest and an inert ingredient used to carry the active ingredient, *e.g.,* solvents or stabilizers. Each product can have one or more inert ingredients—typically their concentration is greater than the active. The identity of the inert is not disclosed on the product label because it is claimed confidential business information by the manufacturers.

The EPA has reviewed the 1200 inerts contained in pesticide products and developed a list of approximately 50 chemicals that cause adverse health effects including cancer, birth defects, and neurotoxicity. Another 50 potentially dangerous chemicals have chemical structures similar to known toxic substances. For approximately 800 inerts, EPA has no information about their potential health effects, and 300 are innocuous.

The EPA has failed to consider the health effects of inert ingredients when regulating pesticides. All pesticides used on food must be issued a tolerance, or an exemption from tolerance. The Agency's regulations clearly state that an exemption from tolerance requirements can only be granted when the "total quantity of the pesticide chemical" in food "will involve no hazard to public health." Yet 15 inerts are carcinogens used on food, and have been exempted from tolerance requirements. These exempted chemicals include benzene, carbon tetrachloride, formaldehyde, methylene chloride, and perchloroethylene. The FDA proposed prohibiting the use of methylene chloride as an aerosol in hair sprays due to its cancer risk.

In early 1987 EPA announced a weak policy regarding inert ingredients. The EPA will "encourage" the removal of inerts listed as hazardous from pesticide products, and may end the use of certain inerts in food use pesticides when sufficient data warranting this action are available.

Inerts can also affect the toxicity of the active ingredient. The largest outbreak of pesticide-caused dermatitis, or skin poisoning, in California occurred because of the inert ingredient in the pesticide product. One hundred fourteen of 198 orange pickers developed dermatitis upon entering citrus orchards treated with Omite-CR, even after the required interval had elapsed between the pesticide spraying and human reentry of the orchards. The poisoning occurred because the pesticide manufacturer used a new inert ingredient that delayed the environmental degradation of the active ingredient. When workers entered the area, residues of the toxic active ingredient were still present.

CELERY

Celery samples had more pesticide residues than any other vegetable in this Guide. Half of the celery analyzed was found to contain residues of one or more pesticides. Twenty-two different pesticides were detected in celery. The EPA has registered approximately 60 different pesticides for use on celery, but FDA's routine laboratory method can detect only 50% of these chemicals. Dicloran residues and chlorothalonil residues were detected in one-quarter of all celery samples. Here are the five pesticides detected most frequently (in order of decreasing occurrence) in fresh celery:

Pesticide	Health effects
Dicloran *DCNA, Botran*	No observed reproductive toxicity in one animal study. According to EPA, has not been sufficiently tested for carcinogenicity, birth defects, or mutagenic effects.
Chlorothalonil *Bravo*	Probable human carcinogen. Some evidence of chronic health effects including kidney, thyroid, stomach and liver changes, and mutagenic effects in laboratory studies. No observed birth defects in animal studies. Hexachlorobenzene contaminant is a probable human carcinogen and is found in food.
Endosulfan *Thiodan*	Some evidence of adverse chronic effects including liver and kidney damage and testicular atrophy in test animals. No observed mutagenic effects in laboratory test systems.
Acephate *Orthene*	Possible human carcinogen. Some evidence of mutagenic effects in laboratory test systems, and reproductive toxicity in one animal study.
Methamidophos *Monitor*	No observed birth defects in one animal study. EPA is reviewing studies submitted to fill previous data gaps for carcinogenicity, birth defects, reproductive toxicity and mutagenic effects.

Can residue be reduced by washing?	Residue reduction
YES	Residues remain on surface following foliar treatment but are absorbed and translocated to edible tissue, following soil treatment. Incorporation of dicloran into wax formulations reduces the effectiveness of washing. Washing, peeling, cooking, or heat processing may reduce residues.
YES	Residues remain primarily on the produce surface; however, chlorothalonil metabolites may be systemic. Washing or cooking reduces residues.
UNKNOWN	Residues remain primarily on the produce surface; however, endosulfan metabolites may be systemic. Peeling, cooking, or heat processing may reduce residues slightly. No information on removal with water.
NO	Residues are systemic and probably cannot be removed with washing. Cooking or canning may reduce residues.
NO	Residues are systemic and probably cannot be removed with washing.

Cutting out pesticides

Trimming the leaves and top of your celery may result in lower levels of residues. The vascular system of celery may act as a sponge by soaking pesticides up the stalk. In one study, methomyl residues decreased 50–90% as a result of trimming.

CHERRIES

H alf of all cherry samples were found to contain residues of one or more pesticides, yet fewer cherry samples were analyzed than any other fruit or vegetable in this Guide. Twenty-five different pesticides were detected in cherries. The EPA has registered over 75 different chemicals for use on cherries, and FDA's routine laboratory method can detect 60% of these chemicals. Parathion and malathion residues were detected in over 20% of all samples. Here are the five pesticides detected most frequently (in order of decreasing occurrence) in fresh cherries:

Pesticide	Health effects
Parathion *Phoskil*	Possible human carcinogen. Some evidence of mutagenic effects in laboratory studies. No observed reproductive toxicity or birth defects in animal studies.
Malathion *Cythion*	Some evidence of reproductive toxicity in the only available animal study. No observed mutagenic effects in available laboratory studies.
Captan *Merpan,* *Orthocide*	Probable human carcinogen. Some evidence of mutagenic effects in laboratory test systems. EPA initiated Special Review in 1980 due to carcinogenicity, mutagenic effects, and presence of residues in food.
Dicloran *DCNA, Botran*	No observed reproductive toxicity in one animal study. According to EPA, has not been sufficiently tested for carcinogenicity, birth defects, or mutagenic effects.
Diazinon *Spectrocide,* *Sarolex*	Some evidence of adverse neurobehavioral effects in the developing offspring of test animals in one study. No observed carcinogenicity or reproductive toxicity in animal studies.

Can residue be reduced by washing?	Residue reduction
UNKNOWN	Residues remain primarily on the produce surface. Washing, peeling, cooking, or heat processing may reduce residues slightly.
YES	Residues remain primarily on the produce surface, but may be absorbed into the peel. Washing with detergent reduces residues more than plain water. Peeling, cooking, or heat processing will reduce residues. Residues on dried fruits were higher than those on fresh fruits because of the concentration effect of dehydration.
YES	Residues remain primarily on the produce surface. However, the metabolite THPI, a suspected carcinogen, may be systemic. Washing, cooking, or heat processing will reduce residues.
YES	Residues remain on surface following foliar treatment. Incorporation of dicloran into wax formulations reduces the effectiveness of washing. Washing, peeling, cooking, or heat processing may reduce residues.
UNKNOWN	Residues remain primarily on the produce surface. Cooking or heat processing may reduce residues. No information on removal with water.

Cosmetic use of pesticides: Are pesticides overused for appearance's sake?

The perfect peach, flawless orange, unblemished tomato and premium cherry are all items that we have come to expect in our supermarkets. What gave these foods this faultless appearance? To be sure, nature had some role in it—but pesticides also play a major part. No one has yet estimated what percentage of pesticide use is for cosmetic purposes. A study in 1976 argued that consumer demand and grower marketing orders can require large amounts of pesticide use. In citrus, the greatest chemical applications are for control of "thrips"—a pest which some insect scientists believe causes only cosmetic damage. Growers also impose their own standards on cosmetic quality—issued in the form of a marketing order—for a particular crop. Then all producers of the crop must meet these standards. Thus consumers have come to expect and demand produce with no visible signs of pest damage. Although the pest damage may pose no health hazard, the chemicals used to produce the perfect-looking food do.

Next time think twice before you reject that blemished fruit.

CORN

Every year, Americans on average eat eleven pounds of corn per person. Less than one percent of the corn analyzed had pesticide residues. The corn husk may prevent pesticide residues from being absorbed into the corn flesh. Eight different pesticides were detected in corn. The FDA's routine laboratory method can detect only 60% of the more than 80 chemicals that can be applied to fresh corn. Here are the five pesticides that were detected most frequently (in order of decreasing occurrence) in fresh corn:

Pesticide	Health effects
Sulfallate *CDEC, Vegadex*	Some evidence of carcinogenicity and mutagenic effects in laboratory studies. Production was discontinued in the U.S. in 1981.
Carbaryl *Sevin*	Some evidence of adverse kidney effects in humans, and mutagenic effects in laboratory test systems. No observed carcinogenicity or reproductive toxicity in animal studies.
Chlorpyrifos *Dursban*	No observed carcinogenicity, birth defects or mutagenic effects in available studies. According to EPA, has not been sufficiently tested for chronic toxicity, carcinogenicity, or mutagenic effects.
Dieldrin	Probable human carcinogen. Causes birth defects and reproductive toxicity in animal studies. Low levels cause adverse effects on learning capabilities in monkeys. EPA cancelled all uses in the U.S. in 1974 due to carcinogenicity, bioaccumulation, and other chronic effects.
Lindane *Agronexit,* *Lindafor,* *Gamma BHC*	Possible human carcinogen. Chronic effects include blood disorders (aplastic anemia) and liver and kidney damage in test animals.

Can residue be reduced by washing?	Residue reduction
UNKNOWN	Sulfallate is not absorbed by foliage but is readily absorbed by roots and then moves through the plant. No information on removal with water.
YES	Residues remain primarily on the produce surface. Washing, peeling, and cooking will reduce residues.
UNKNOWN	Residues remain primarily on the produce surface. No information on removal with water. Dried fruits showed higher levels of residues than on fresh fruits because of the concentration effect of dehydration.
UNKNOWN	Residues remain primarily on the produce surface. No information on removal with water. Peeling or cooking may reduce residues.
UNKNOWN	Some evidence that residues are systemic. No information on removal with water.

Pesticides where they don't belong

There were only eight pesticides detected in corn by FDA and CDFA from 1982 to 1985. Besides the five listed in the table, acephate, aldrin, and EDB were also detected. Each of these eight pesticide residues only showed up once in all of the samples analyzed. Of these eight pesticides, two (aldrin and dieldrin) were cancelled by EPA in 1974, another (EDB) was cancelled by EPA in 1984, and one (sulfallate) was discontinued by the manufacturer in 1981. Finally, two chemicals (lindane and acephate) are not permitted for use on corn—in other words, the presence of these residues is illegal. While the residues were all in very small amounts, this is a good example of the wide range of residues that can be present on a particular crop.

The alachlor story

Alachlor, or Lasso, is the most widely used herbicide in the nation; use is estimated at 80–84 million pounds per year mainly on corn, soybeans, and peanuts. Thirty-five percent of the United States corn crop is treated with alachlor each year. Based on feeding studies in rats and mice, EPA has classified alachlor as a probable human carcinogen. Alachlor has been detected in the groundwater in nine states, so consumers may also be exposed to it in their drinking water. Very little information exists to determine the levels of alachlor residues in food because FDA's routine laboratory methods cannot detect the chemical. The EPA proposed minimal restrictions on alachlor use in October 1986; these rules became final in December 1987.

CUCUMBERS

Half of all cucumbers sampled were found to contain residues of one or more pesticides, and 80% of imported cucumbers had residues. Thirty-two different pesticides were detected in cucumbers. The EPA has registered more than 75 different pesticides for use on cucumbers, and FDA's routine laboratory method can detect approximately 60% of these chemicals. Methamidophos residues were detected in one-third of the samples analyzed. Here are the five pesticides detected most frequently (in order of decreasing occurrence) in fresh cucumbers:

Pesticide	Health effects
Methamidophos *Monitor*	No observed birth defects in one animal study. EPA is reviewing studies submitted to fill previous data gaps for carcinogenicity, birth defects, reproductive toxicity and mutagenic effects.
Endosulfan *Thiodan*	Some evidence of adverse chronic effects including liver and kidney damage and testicular atrophy in test animals. No observed mutagenic effects in laboratory test systems.
Dieldrin	Probable human carcinogen. Causes birth defects and reproductive toxicity in animal studies. Low levels cause adverse effects on learning capabilities in monkeys. EPA cancelled all uses in the U.S. in 1974 due to carcinogenicity, bioaccumulation, and other chronic effects.
Chlorpyrifos *Dursban*	No observed carcinogenicity, birth defects or mutagenic effects in available studies. According to EPA, has not been sufficiently tested for chronic toxicity, carcinogenicity, or mutagenic effects.
Dimethoate *Cygon, Rogon*	Some evidence of carcinogenicity, birth defects, reproductive toxicity and mutagenic effects in laboratory studies.

Can residue be reduced by washing?	Residue reduction
NO	Residues are systemic and probably cannot be removed with washing.
UNKNOWN	Residues remain primarily on the produce surface; however, endosulfan metabolites may be systemic. Peeling may reduce residues slightly. No information on removal with water.
UNKNOWN	Residues remain primarily on the produce surface. No information on removal with water. Peeling may reduce residues.
UNKNOWN	Residues remain primarily on the produce surface. No information on removal with water.
UNKNOWN	Residues are systemic. However, washing and peeling reduced residues in various studies.

Cucumber production in the United States

Nearly 150,000 acres of cucumbers are grown throughout the United States, with major production in Florida, California, Texas, and South Carolina. Of the 13 chemicals that are used most extensively in cucumber production, at least seven have been linked to cancer in animal studies. Further, only eight of these 13 chemicals can be detected by FDA's routine laboratory methods.

Imported cucumbers

Cucumbers and pickles were imported into the United States from a total of 50 countries between 1983 and 1985, and from 27 countries in each year. However, FDA annually sampled shipments of cucumbers from only nine out of the 27 countries. Furthermore, cucumbers from 17 of these 50 countries were not sampled in any of the years from 1979 to 1985, including the country producing the second largest volume of imports.

There were at least ten shipments of Mexican cucumbers with illegal pesticide residues detected by FDA's Los Angeles laboratory in 1986. For five of these shipments, the importer was allowed to redirect them to another country with less stringent restrictions.

Imports accounted for 78% of the cucumbers analyzed by FDA, and 80% of these samples contained residues. By contrast, only 30% of the domestic cucumbers FDA analyzed contained residues.

GRAPEFRUIT

One-fifth of the grapefruit samples were found to contain residues of one or more pesticides. This is about the same level of contamination that was found in oranges. Fifteen different pesticides were detected in grapefruit. The EPA has registered more than 80 different pesticides for use on grapefruit, and FDA's routine laboratory method can detect 60% of these chemicals. Here are the five pesticides detected most frequently (in order of decreasing occurrence) in fresh grapefruit:

Pesticide	Health effects
Thiabendazole *TBZ, Mertect*	No observed carcinogenicity or birth defects in test animals.
Ethion *Ethanox,* *Ethiol,* *Rhodocide*	EPA is reviewing studies submitted to fill previous data gaps for carcinogenicity, birth defects, reproductive toxicity and mutagenic effects.
Methidathion *Supracide,* *Somonil*	Some evidence of carcinogenicity in animal studies. No observed mutagenic effects in laboratory test systems. According to EPA, has not been sufficiently tested for carcinogenicity, birth defects or reproductive toxicity.
Chlorobenzilate *Acaraben*	Causes cancer in animal studies. Some evidence of reproductive toxicity, including adverse testicular effects in test animals. Contaminated with DDT. In 1979 EPA cancelled all uses in the U.S. due to carcinogenicity and reproductive toxicity *except* on citrus.
Carbaryl *Sevin*	Some evidence of adverse kidney effects in humans, and mutagenic effects in laboratory test systems. No observed carcinogenicity or reproductive toxicity in animal studies.

Can residue be reduced by washing?	Residue reduction
YES	Residues are primarily found in the peel. Peeling or washing will reduce residues.
YES	Residues remain primarily on the produce surface. Washing or processing may reduce residues.
UNKNOWN	Residues remain primarily in the peel of citrus fruit. No information on removal with water.
YES	Residues remain primarily on the citrus peel. Washing and processing of citrus fruit will reduce residues.
YES	Residues remain primarily on the produce surface. Washing or peeling will reduce residues.

The EDB story

Ethylene dibromide (EDB) was an insecticide with many uses. As a soil fumigant, EDB controlled nematodes—microscopic worms that attack plant roots. In post-harvest grain fumigation EDB controlled insects, and in post-harvest fruit and vegetable fumigation EDB controlled fruit flies. In 1984 EPA cancelled all uses of EDB, except as a post-harvest fumigant on citrus to be exported to Japan, due to its carcinogenicity, mutagenicity and reproductive toxicity. EDB residues cannot be detected by FDA or CDFA's normal laboratory tests. Nevertheless, 17% of the grapefruit analyzed by FDA and CDFA with special tests in 1984 had EDB residues. Although EDB has been used as a pesticide since the 1950s, its use sharply increased in 1979 after a similar product, DBCP, was banned. Consumers were alerted to the hazards of EDB in 1983 and 1984 when high levels of residues were discovered in flour and packaged cake mixes. EDB residues in our food are not likely to continue in the future because all domestic uses have been cancelled. Residues in foods imported from other nations are not permitted because all tolerances, except on mangoes, have been revoked.

GRAPES

One-third of the grapes analyzed were found to contain residues of one or more pesticides. Thirty different pesticides were detected in grapes. The EPA has registered more than 80 different pesticides for use on grapes, but FDA's routine laboratory method can detect fewer than 60% of these chemicals. Captan residues were detected in 15% of all samples, and dimethoate residues were found in 20% of the samples analyzed by FDA. Here are the five pesticides detected most frequently (in order of decreasing occurrence) in fresh grapes:

Pesticide	Health effects
Captan *Merpan, Orthocide*	Probable human carcinogen. Some evidence of mutagenic effects in laboratory test systems. EPA initiated Special Review in 1980 due to carcinogenicity, mutagenic effects, and presence of residues in food.
Dimethoate *Cygon, Rogon*	Some evidence of carcinogenicity, birth defects, reproductive toxicity and mutagenic effects in laboratory studies.
Dicloran *DCNA, Botran*	No observed reproductive toxicity in one animal study. According to EPA, has not been sufficiently tested for carcinogenicity, birth defects, or mutagenic effects.
Carbaryl *Sevin*	Some evidence of adverse kidney effects in humans, and mutagenic effects in laboratory test systems. No observed carcinogenicity or reproductive toxicity in animal studies.
Iprodione *Rovral*	Some evidence of adverse health effects including liver, urinary and immune system damage, and mutagenic effects in laboratory studies. No observed birth defects in animal studies.

Can residue be reduced by washing?	Residue reduction
YES	Residues remain primarily on the produce surface. However, the metabolite THPI, a suspected carcinogen, may be systemic. Washing, cooking, or heat processing will reduce residues. Wine made from captan-treated grapes had no residues in one study.
UNKNOWN	Residues are systemic. However, washing, peeling, cooking, or heat processing reduced residues in various studies.
YES	Residues remain on surface following foliar treatment. Incorporation of dicloran into wax formulations reduces the effectiveness of washing. Washing, peeling, cooking, or heat processing may reduce residues.
YES	Residues remain primarily on the produce surface. Washing, peeling, or cooking will reduce residues.
UNKNOWN	Residues remain primarily on the produce surface. No information on removal with water.

Imported grapes

Imports of grapes to the United States increased by 113 percent from 1982 to 1986. Nearly 450,000 tons of grapes were imported in 1986. Imports accounted for 68% of the grapes analyzed by FDA, and 44% of these samples contained pesticide residues. In contrast, 28% of domestically-grown grapes had detectable levels of pesticides.

GREEN BEANS

E very year, Americans on average eat 11 pounds of green beans per person. One-quarter of all green beans sampled were found to contain residues of one or more pesticides, and nearly half of all imported green beans analyzed contained residues. Thirty-two different pesticides were detected in green beans. The EPA has registered more than 60 different chemicals for use on green beans, and FDA's routine laboratory method can detect only 60% of these chemicals. Dimethoate and methamidophos residues were detected in over ten percent of the FDA samples. Here are the five pesticides detected most frequently (in order of decreasing occurrence) in fresh green beans:

Pesticide	Health effects
Dimethoate *Cygon, Rogon*	Some evidence of carcinogenicity, birth defects, reproductive toxicity and mutagenic effects in laboratory studies.
Methamidophos *Monitor*	No observed birth defects in one animal study. EPA is reviewing studies submitted to fill previous data gaps for carcinogenicity, birth defects, reproductive toxicity and mutagenic effects.
Endosulfan *Thiodan*	Some evidence of adverse chronic effects including liver and kidney damage and testicular atrophy in test animals. No observed mutagenic effects in laboratory test systems.
Acephate *Orthene*	Possible human carcinogen. Some evidence of mutagenic effects in laboratory test systems, and reproductive toxicity in one animal study.
Chlorothalonil *Bravo*	Probable human carcinogen. Some evidence of chronic health effects including kidney, thyroid, stomach and liver changes, and mutagenic effects in laboratory studies. No observed birth defects in animal studies. Hexachlorobenzene contaminant is a probable human carcinogen and is found in food.

Can residue be reduced by washing?	Residue reduction
UNKNOWN	Residues are systemic. However, washing, peeling, cooking, or heat processing reduced residues in various studies.
NO	Residues are systemic and probably cannot be removed with washing.
UNKNOWN	Residues remain primarily on the produce surface; however, endosulfan metabolites may be systemic. Peeling, cooking, or heat processing may reduce residues slightly. No information on removal with water.
NO	Residues are systemic and probably cannot be removed with washing. Cooking or canning may reduce residues.
YES	Residues remain primarily on the produce surface; however, chlorothalonil metabolites may be systemic. Washing or cooking reduces residues.

Food can be sold before
FDA completes residue analysis

The FDA allows some shipments of perishable food to immediately enter the channels of trade without waiting for samples to be analyzed. Generally, there are three conditions that allow importers to distribute fresh produce: (1) there is no reason to suspect that the product contains illegal pesticide residues, (2) the product would deteriorate or spoil before the analysis was completed, and (3) the importer agrees to attempt to retrieve the distributed shipment if the sample is found to be adulterated.

Two shipments of green beans from Mexico with illegal pesticide residues were detected by FDA's Los Angeles laboratory in 1986. Neither of these shipments were retrieved because they were allowed to be sold in supermarkets before the results of the sample analysis were known.

LETTUCE

Every year, Americans on average eat 11 pounds of lettuce per person. One-third of the lettuce sampled was found to contain residues of one or more pesticides. Lettuce was the most frequently sampled food included in this Guide. Forty-three different pesticides were detected in lettuce. The laboratory method routinely used by the federal government can only detect approximately 60% of the more than 60 chemicals that can be applied to lettuce. Mevinphos was found in 19% of the lettuce analyzed by FDA. Here are the five pesticides detected most frequently (in order of decreasing occurrence) in fresh lettuce:

Pesticide	Health effects
Mevinphos *Phosdrin*	Some evidence of mutagenic effects in one available study. No observed carcinogenicity, reproductive toxicity or birth defects in animal studies. According to EPA, has not been sufficiently tested for carcinogenicity.
Endosulfan *Thiodan*	Some evidence of adverse chronic effects including liver and kidney damage and testicular atrophy in test animals. No observed mutagenic effects in laboratory test systems.
Permethrin *Ambush, Pounce*	Possible human carcinogen. Some evidence of reproductive toxicity in one animal study. No observed birth defects or mutagenic effects in laboratory studies.
Dimethoate *Cygon, Rogon*	Some evidence of carcinogenicity, birth defects, reproductive toxicity and mutagenic effects in laboratory studies.
Methomyl *Lannate*	Some evidence of adverse chronic health effects including kidney, spleen and blood changes in animal studies. Some evidence of mutagenic effects in one laboratory test system. No observed carcinogenicity, birth defects, or reproductive toxicity in available animal studies.

Can residue be reduced by washing?	Residue reduction
NO	Residues are systemic and probably cannot be removed with washing.
UNKNOWN	Residues remain primarily on the produce surface; however, endosulfan metabolites may be systemic. No information on removal with water.
YES	Residues remain primarily on the produce surface. Washing with detergent will reduce residues; plain water may not.
UNKNOWN	Residues are systemic. However, washing and peeling reduced residues in various studies.
NO	Residues are systemic and probably cannot be removed with washing.

The EBDCs

The EBDCs, or ethylene bisdithiocarbamates, are the most widely used group of fungicides in the United States. These chemicals comprise approximately 22% of all fungicides used in the United States and 57% of the total fungicide use worldwide. Roughly one-third of all fruits and vegetables grown in the U.S. are treated with EBDCs. The primary crops treated with EBDCs are apples, grapes, potatoes, sweet corn, tomatoes, onions, and citrus. Despite this widespread usage, only minimal data exist to determine the presence of EBDC residues in food because these chemicals cannot be routinely detected by the federal and state monitoring programs.

Both through environmental degradation and the application of heat in cooking or food processing, the EBDCs are known to break down into ethylenethiourea (ETU), a probable human carcinogen. In several separate cancer studies, ETU and the EBDCs were shown to cause liver, lung, and thyroid tumors. EPA documents also show that the EBDCs and ETU may cause birth defects and genetic mutations.

The EPA placed these chemicals into RPAR, an extensive investigation of a compound's hazards, in 1977 because of concerns about the risks of cancer, birth defects and toxicity to aquatic organisms. Following five private meetings with the manufacturers of the pesticides (duPont and Rohm and Haas), EPA terminated the RPAR. Use of the chemicals was allowed to continue virtually unrestricted.

In 1983, NRDC and the AFL-CIO filed suit against EPA for its practice of holding private meetings with pesticide manufacturers concerning the regulation of their products. As settlement, the court ordered EPA to reassess previous decisions on several chemicals, including the EBDCs by December 31, 1986. On December 30, 1986, EPA requested an extension of the reassessment deadline until March 30, 1990—over three years—because data on the presence of EBDCs and ETU in food were not available.

The NRDC did not accept the requested delay of the reassessment and urged the Agency to take swifter action. As a result, EPA formally returned the EBDCs to Special Review in July 1987 because of concern about the potential cancer risk for consumers of foods treated with EBDCs. A final decision about whether the EBDCs should continue to be used on food will not be reached for several years. Pending further testing, these hazardous chemicals are still being widely used on food but FDA does not regularly test for their presence in food.

ONIONS

Every year, Americans on average eat over five pounds of onions per person. Ten percent of the onions sampled were found to contain residues of one or more pesticides. Eighteen different pesticides were detected in onions. The EPA has registered 50 different chemicals for use on onions, and FDA's routine laboratory method can detect fewer than 60% of these chemicals. DDT residues were detected in over 10% of FDA's onion samples. Here are the five pesticides detected most frequently (in order of decreasing occurrence) in fresh onions:

Pesticide	Health effects
DCPA *Dacthal,* *Chlorthal-* *dimethyl*	No observed birth defects in laboratory studies. According to EPA, has not been sufficiently tested for carcinogenicity or mutagenic effects.
DDT	Probable human carcinogen. Some evidence of reproductive toxicity, and adverse liver effects in animal studies. EPA cancelled all uses in the U.S. in 1972 due to carcinogenicity, bioaccumulation, and other chronic effects.
Ethion *Ethanox, Ethiol,* *Rhodocide*	EPA is reviewing studies submitted to fill previous data gaps for carcinogenicity, birth defects, reproductive toxicity and mutagenic effects.
Diazinon *Spectrocide,* *Sarolex*	Some evidence of adverse neurobehavioral effects in the developing offspring of test animals in one study. No observed carcinogenicity or reproductive toxicity in animal studies.
Malathion *Cythion*	Some evidence of reproductive toxicity in the only available animal study. No observed mutagenic effects in available laboratory studies.

Can residue be reduced by washing?	Residue reduction
UNKNOWN	Some evidence that residues are systemic. For a preemergence herbicide, the relatively frequent findings of residues indicate a fair degree of persistence. No information on removal with water.
YES	Residues remain primarily on the produce surface, although residues may be absorbed into the peel. Washing, cooking, and commercial processing will reduce residues to some extent in spinach. Washing and peeling reduce residues in root crops, but cooking won't reduce residues once they have been absorbed into the plant tissue.
YES	Residues remain primarily on the produce surface. Washing or processing may reduce residues.
UNKNOWN	Residues remain primarily on the produce surface. Cooking or heat processing may reduce residues. No information on removal with water.
YES	Residues remain primarily on the produce surface, but may be absorbed into the peel. Washing with detergent reduces residues more than plain water. Peeling, cooking, or heat processing will reduce residues. Residues on dried fruits were higher than those on fresh fruits because of the concentration effect of dehydration.

Imported onions

Imports of onions to the United States increased by 51% from 1982 to 1986. Over 700 million pounds of onions were imported into the United States from 1983–1985, and 240 million pounds of onions were imported in 1986. The United States imports onions from 46 countries.

# ORANGES

E very year, Americans on average eat over seven pounds of oranges per person. One-fifth of the oranges sampled were found to contain residues of one or more pesticides, and nearly half of all imported oranges had residues. Thirty different pesticides were detected in oranges. The EPA has registered nearly 90 different chemicals for use on oranges, but FDA's routine laboratory method can detect only 50% of these pesticides. Here are the five pesticides detected most frequently (in order of decreasing occurrence) in fresh oranges:

Pesticide	Health effects
Methidathion *Supracide,* *Somonil*	Some evidence of carcinogenicity in animal studies. No observed mutagenic effects in laboratory test systems. According to EPA, has not been sufficiently tested for carcinogenicity, birth defects or reproductive toxicity.
Chlorpyrifos *Dursban*	No observed carcinogenicity, birth defects or mutagenic effects in available studies. According to EPA, has not been sufficiently tested for chronic toxicity, carcinogenicity, or mutagenic effects.
Ethion *Ethanox, Ethiol,* *Rhodocide*	EPA is reviewing studies submitted to fill previous data gaps for carcinogenicity, birth defects, reproductive toxicity and mutagenic effects.
Parathion *Phoskil*	Possible human carcinogen. Some evidence of mutagenic effects in laboratory studies. No observed reproductive toxicity or birth defects in animal studies.
Carbaryl *Sevin*	Some evidence of adverse kidney effects in humans, and mutagenic effects in laboratory test systems. No observed carcinogenicity or reproductive toxicity in animal studies.

Can residue be reduced by washing?	Residue reduction
UNKNOWN	Residues remain primarily in the peel of citrus fruit. No information on removal with water.
UNKNOWN	Residues remain primarily on the produce surface. No information on removal with water.
YES	Residues remain primarily on the produce surface. Washing or processing may reduce residues.
UNKNOWN	Residues remain primarily on the produce surface. Washing, peeling, cooking, or heat processing may reduce residues slightly.
YES	Residues remain primarily on the produce surface. Washing, peeling, or cooking will reduce residues.

Imported oranges

Imports of oranges to the United States increased by 100% from 1982 to 1986. Over 60 million pounds of oranges were imported in 1986. Imports accounted for 26% of FDA's samples, and 49% of these samples contained pesticides. In contrast, 36% of FDA's domestic oranges analyzed contained residues.

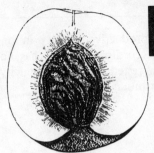# PEACHES

O ver half of all fresh peaches sampled were found to contain residues of one or more pesticides. Peaches contained more pesticide residues than any other fruit or vegetable in this Guide, except for strawberries. Every year, Americans on average eat ten pounds of peaches per person. Thirty-six different pesticides were detected in peaches. The routine laboratory method used by the federal government can only detect 55% of the nearly 100 pesticides that can be applied to peaches. Dicloran residues were detected in 30% of all samples, and captan residues were detected in 20% of the FDA samples. Here are the five pesticides detected most frequently (in order of decreasing occurrence) in fresh peaches:

Pesticide	Health effects
Dicloran *DCNA, Botran*	No observed reproductive toxicity in one animal study. According to EPA, has not been sufficiently tested for carcinogenicity, birth defects, or mutagenic effects.
Captan *Merpan,* *Orthocide*	Probable human carcinogen. Some evidence of mutagenic effects in laboratory test systems. EPA initiated Special Review in 1980 due to carcinogenicity, mutagenic effects, and presence of residues in food.
Parathion *Phoskil*	Possible human carcinogen. Some evidence of mutagenic effects in laboratory studies. No observed reproductive toxicity or birth defects in animal studies.
Carbaryl *Sevin*	Some evidence of adverse kidney effects in humans, and mutagenic effects in laboratory test systems. No observed carcinogenicity or reproductive toxicity in animal studies.
Endosulfan *Thiodan*	Some evidence of adverse chronic effects including liver and kidney damage and testicular atrophy in test animals. No observed mutagenic effects in laboratory test systems.

Can residue be reduced by washing?	Residue reduction
YES	Residues remain on surface following foliar treatment but are absorbed and translocated to edible tissue, following soil treatment. Incorporation of dicloran into wax formulations reduces the effectiveness of washing. Washing, peeling, cooking, or heat processing may reduce residues.
YES	Residues remain primarily on the produce surface. However, the metabolite THPI, a suspected carcinogen, may be systemic. Washing, cooking, or heat processing will reduce residues.
UNKNOWN	Residues remain primarily on the produce surface. Washing, peeling, cooking, or heat processing may reduce residues slightly.
YES	Residues remain primarily on the produce surface. Washing, peeling, or cooking will reduce residues.
UNKNOWN	Residues remain primarily on the produce surface; however, endosulfan metabolites may be systemic. Peeling, cooking, or heat processing may reduce residues slightly. No information on removal with water.

Imported peaches

Imported fresh fruits now account for 25% of the total United States fruit supply. Nearly 260,000 pounds of peaches were imported from 42 countries between 1983 and 1985. Imports accounted for only 11% of the peach samples analyzed by FDA, but nearly 60% of these contained pesticide residues.

The benomyl story

Benomyl, or Benlate, is a systemic fungicide that is widely used in the United States on 43 food crops. The EPA has classified benomyl as a possible human carcinogen. Benomyl causes birth defects and reproductive toxicity (decreased sperm count) in test animals. It is also mutagenic in some laboratory test systems.

Fifty percent to 75% of the peaches grown in the United States are treated with benomyl. However, FDA's routine laboratory test cannot detect benomyl. Therefore, very few food samples were identified as containing benomyl residues—despite its widespread use. A special analytical method to detect benomyl is available though rarely used. Since benomyl is systemic and gets inside the fruit, you can't wash the residues off. In addition, there is some evidence that residues are greater in processed foods because concentration of the pesticide occurs during processing, such as in orange juice, dried apricots, dried prunes, and grape juice.

PEARS

Every year, Americans on average eat six pounds of pears per person. One-fifth of all pears sampled were found to contain residues of one or more pesticides. Twenty-seven different pesticides were detected in pears. The EPA has registered nearly 100 different pesticides for use on pears, and FDA's routine laboratory method can detect only approximately 50% of these chemicals. Azinphos-methyl and cyhexatin residues were detected in over ten percent of FDA's samples. Here are the five pesticides detected most frequently (in order of decreasing occurrence) in fresh pears:

Pesticide	Health effects
Azinphos-methyl *Guthion*	EPA is reviewing studies submitted to fill previous data gaps for carcinogenicity, birth defects, reproductive toxicity, and mutagenic effects.
Cyhexatin *Plictran*	Causes birth defects in animal studies (see page 110). Some evidence of adverse health effects in the liver in test animals. No observed carcinogenicity or mutagenic effects in laboratory studies.
Phosmet *Imidan*	Possible human carcinogen. Some evidence of mutagenic effects in laboratory test systems and humans (pesticide factory workers). No observed birth defects or reproductive toxicity in animal studies.
Endosulfan *Thiodan*	Some evidence of adverse chronic effects including liver and kidney damage and testicular atrophy in test animals. No observed mutagenic effects in laboratory test systems.
Ethion *Ethanox, Ethiol,* *Rhodocide*	EPA is reviewing studies submitted to fill previous data gaps for carcinogenicity, birth defects, reproductive toxicity and mutagenic effects.

Can residue be reduced by washing?	Residue reduction
YES	Residues remain primarily on the produce surface. Washing, cooking, or heat processing will reduce residues.
UNKNOWN	Residues remain primarily on the produce surface. Cyhexatin does not readily dissolve in water. Therefore, plain water washing may not reduce residues, but peeling may help. Residues in processed fruits are greater than in fresh fruits.
YES	Residues remain primarily on the produce surface. Washing or cooking will reduce residues.
UNKNOWN	Residues remain primarily on the produce surface; however, endosulfan metabolites may be systemic. Peeling, cooking, or heat processing may reduce residues slightly. No information on removal with water.
YES	Residues remain primarily on the produce surface. Washing or processing may reduce residues.

State suspends hazardous pesticide

On June 24, 1987, the California Department of Food and Agriculture (CDFA) announced the suspension of the pesticide Plictran (cyhexatin). The announcement stated that, "pesticides containing cyhexatin may result in birth defects or toxicity in female workers who mix, load, apply, or are exposed to residues on the crops for which it is registered." It is very unusual for a state to take such immediate action without any previous actions by EPA. In the press release, CDFA also stated that they planned to test crops in the field and at markets to insure that food residues remained within safe limits. A month later, EPA issued a warning that "exposure of pregnant women to the pesticide cyhexatin during application or while working in fields where it has been applied may pose a risk of birth defects to their unborn children." By September 1987, the two registrants, Dow Chemical and Chevron, had requested voluntary cancellation of their cyhexatin registrations, had initiated recalls of all remaining stocks from channels of trade, and had halted all production of cyhexatin worldwide. The EPA granted the voluntary cancellation to be effective December 31, 1987.

Baam or bust?

Amitraz, or Baam, is an insecticide that is probably used on 40% to 50% of the pears grown in the United States. However, it cannot be detected by the laboratory methods routinely used by FDA. Therefore, very few pear samples were identified as containing amitraz. Although a special test exists to detect residues, federal and state government laboratories rarely use this test. The EPA has classified amitraz as a possible human carcinogen based on animal studies.

POTATOES

E very year, Americans on average eat over 54 pounds of fresh potatoes per person. One-fifth of the potatoes sampled were found to contain residues of one or more pesticides. Thirty-eight different pesticides were detected in potatoes. The EPA has registered almost 90 different pesticides for use on potatoes, and FDA's routine laboratory method can detect only approximately 55% of these chemicals. Here are the five pesticides detected most frequently (in order of decreasing occurrence) in fresh potatoes:

Pesticide	Health effects
DDT	Probable human carcinogen. Some evidence of reproductive toxicity, and adverse liver effects in animal studies. EPA cancelled all uses in the U.S. in 1972 due to carcinogenicity, bioaccumulation, and other chronic effects.
Chlorpropham *CIPC*	Some evidence of mutagenic effects in laboratory test systems. Has not been sufficiently tested for cancer.
Dieldrin	Probable human carcinogen. Causes birth defects and reproductive toxicity in animal studies. Low levels cause adverse effects on learning capabilities in monkeys. EPA cancelled all uses in the U.S. in 1974 due to carcinogenicity, bioaccumulation, and other chronic effects.
Aldicarb *Temik*	Capable of causing severe poisoning at very small doses. Some evidence that it can cause changes in the immune system of humans. EPA initiated Special Review in 1984 due to aldicarb's acute toxicity and presence of residues in food.
Chlordane *Octachlor, Velsicol 1068*	Probable human carcinogen. Some evidence of birth defects, reproductive toxicity, and mutagenic effects in laboratory studies. EPA cancelled agricultural uses in the U.S. in 1978, and interior home use to control termites in 1987. Residues persist in body tissues and the environment.

Can residue be reduced by washing?	Residue reduction
YES	Residues remain primarily on the produce surface, although residues may be absorbed into the peel. Washing and peeling reduce residues in potatoes, but cooking won't reduce residues once they have been absorbed into the plant tissue.
NO	Residues are primarily systemic and probably cannot be removed with washing.
UNKNOWN	Residues remain primarily on the produce surface, although there is some evidence that residues are systemic in root crops. No information on removal with water. Peeling or cooking may reduce residues.
NO	Residues are systemic and probably cannot be removed with washing. Cooking or heat processing may reduce residues.
UNKNOWN	Residues remain primarily on the produce surface, although there is some evidence that residues are systemic in root crops. No information on removal with water.

Persistent pesticides

Three of the five most frequently detected pesticides on potatoes have been banned from use on food grown in the United States since 1978 (DDT, dieldrin, chlordane). These residues are probably occurring because small amounts of these chemicals have persisted in the environment, particularly the soil. Other possible sources of these residues could be illegal use of the cancelled chemicals or continued use of the chemicals in foreign nations that export food to the United States.

Work is hazardous

While pesticide residues in food may pose a serious health risk for consumers, the risks generally are far greater for field workers. Many pesticides can cause illness, or acute toxicity, immediately or up to several weeks after exposure. This creates a hazard for workers who are frequently exposed to pesticides during their application or when they enter fields after pesticide treatments. Typically, residues in the food sold in the supermarket are lower than levels in the field. For example, EPA initially stopped all uses of the chemical dinoseb in October 1986 because of the potential risks for workers of birth defects, male sterility, and possibly cancer. As a result of pressure from growers, EPA then allowed certain dinoseb uses to continue for two more years. Dinoseb was used on 50% of the potato crop before the suspension, as well as on dried beans and peas, berries, cucumbers, melons and green beans. Dinoseb residues are probably not a hazard for consumers because it is not used on the edible portion of plants and residues disappear from food rapidly. But workers in fields that have been treated with dinoseb are at risk.

California currently has the nation's strongest program—even tougher than EPA—to protect farm workers from pesticides. In spite of this effort, reported pesticide poisonings among workers have risen an average 14% a year since 1973. The number of reported cases doubled between 1975 and 1985. Fieldhands currently suffer the highest rates of occupational illness in the state.

SPINACH

Twenty-nine percent of all spinach sampled was found to contain residues of one or more pesticides. Overall, the occurrence of pesticide residues in spinach is about the same as in lettuce. Twenty-nine different pesticides were detected in spinach. The EPA has registered more than 50 pesticides for use on spinach, but FDA's routine laboratory method can detect only 55% of these chemicals. Here are the five pesticides detected most frequently (in order of decreasing occurrence) in fresh spinach:

Pesticide	Health effects
Endosulfan *Thiodan*	Some evidence of adverse chronic effects including liver and kidney damage and testicular atrophy in test animals. No observed mutagenic effects in laboratory test systems.
DDT	Probable human carcinogen. Some evidence of reproductive toxicity, and adverse liver effects in animal studies. EPA cancelled all uses in the U.S. in 1972 due to carcinogenicity, bioaccumulation, and other chronic effects.
Methomyl *Lannate*	Some evidence of adverse chronic health effects including kidney, spleen and blood changes observed in animal studies. Some evidence of mutagenic effects in one laboratory test system. No observed carcinogenicity, birth defects, or reproductive toxicity in available animal studies.
Methamidophos *Monitor*	No observed birth defects in one animal study. EPA is reviewing studies submitted to fill previous data gaps for carcinogenicity, birth defects, reproductive toxicity and mutagenic effects.
Dimethoate *Cygon, Rogon*	Some evidence of carcinogenicity, birth defects, reproductive toxicity and mutagenic effects in laboratory studies.

Can residue be reduced by washing?	Residue reduction
UNKNOWN	Residues remain primarily on the produce surface; however, endosulfan metabolites may be systemic. Cooking or heat processing may reduce residues slightly. No information on removal with water.
YES	Residues remain primarily on the produce surface, although residues may be absorbed into the peel. Washing, cooking, and commercial processing will reduce residues to some extent in spinach.
NO	Residues are systemic and probably cannot be removed with washing. Residues are stable at freezing temperatures; however, cooking or heat processing will reduce residues.
NO	Residues are systemic and probably cannot be removed with washing. Residues remain primarily in the outer leaves of lettuce, so stripping these tough layers in spinach may reduce residues.
UNKNOWN	Residues are systemic. However, washing, cooking, and heat processing reduced residues in various studies.

Dirty pesticides

The health hazards of pesticides are not only due to the active ingredients. For example, the active ingredient methomyl may have a breakdown product—or "metabolite"—called acetamide which has been shown to be a possible human carcinogen, even though methomyl itself has not caused cancer in several studies. The pesticide captan has a metabolite THPI that EPA is concerned may also be a carcinogen. Pesticide products also contain contaminants (unintended byproducts of the manufacturing process) that may be much more hazardous than the pesticide. The following chart shows some common carcinogenic contaminants of pesticides:

Pesticide	Contaminant
Trifluralin, Dicamba	Nitrosamines
PCNB (*Quintozene*), Tecnazene, Chlorothalonil	Hexachlorobenzene (HCB)
Chlorobenzilate, Dicofol	DDT
2,4,5-T	TCDD (dioxin)
Diazinon	Sulfotepp

STRAWBERRIES

More pesticide residues were detected in strawberries than in any fruit or vegetable in this Guide. Over 60% of strawberries sampled were found to contain residues of one or more pesticides. In fact, 86% of the imported strawberry samples had pesticide residues. Thirty-nine different pesticides were detected in strawberries. The EPA has registered more than 70 different pesticides for use on strawberries, and about 50% of these can be routinely detected by FDA. Captan residues were detected on one-third of all the strawberries analyzed. Here are the five pesticides detected most frequently (in order of decreasing occurrence) in fresh strawberries:

Pesticide	Health effects
Captan *Merpan, Orthocide*	Probable human carcinogen. Some evidence of mutagenic effects in laboratory test systems. EPA initiated Special Review in 1980 due to carcinogenicity, mutagenic effects, and presence of residues in food.
Vinclozolin *Ronilan*	Some evidence of mutagenic effects in one laboratory test system. No observed birth defects in the only available studies.
Endosulfan *Thiodan*	Some evidence of adverse chronic effects including liver and kidney damage and testicular atrophy in test animals. No observed mutagenic effects in laboratory test systems.
Methamidophos *Monitor*	No observed birth defects in one animal study. EPA is reviewing studies submitted to fill previous data gaps for carcinogenicity, birth defects, reproductive toxicity and mutagenic effects.
Methyl Parathion *Folidol M, Metacide*	Some evidence of carcinogenicity and adverse chronic health effects including blood changes in animal studies. Some evidence of mutagenic effects in laboratory test systems. According to EPA, has not been sufficiently tested for carcinogenicity or birth defects.

Can residue be reduced by washing?	Residue reduction
YES	Residues remain primarily on the produce surface. However, the metabolite THPI, a suspected carcinogen, may be systemic. Washing, cooking, or heat processing will reduce residues.
UNKNOWN	Residues remain primarily on the produce surface, but some evidence that residues can be absorbed. Cooking or heat processing will reduce residues.
UNKNOWN	Residues remain primarily on the produce surface; however, endosulfan metabolites may be systemic. Cooking or heat processing may reduce residues slightly. No information on removal with water.
NO	Residues are systemic and probably cannot be removed with washing.
UNKNOWN	Residues remain primarily on the produce surface, but some evidence that residues can be absorbed. No information on removal with water.

Circle of poison

Imported fresh fruits account for 25% of the total U.S. supply, and approximately 6% of the nation's fresh vegetables are imports. Imported products pose a unique hazard to the safety of the American food supply. The use of pesticides on food in other countries is not governed by United States regulations, but instead by the laws of the nation producing the food. Many food-exporting nations in the developing world lack strict pesticide regulations, and farmers are often untrained in safe and proper agrichemical uses. Hundreds of pesticides are exported from the United States and other developed countries for use throughout the world. Some of these exported pesticides have been banned or, alternatively, never registered in developed nations. United States consumers are exposed to residues of these banned or unregulated chemicals in imported foods sold in this country. Imports accounted for 24% of the strawberries analyzed by FDA from 1982 to 1985 and 86% of these had residues. In contrast, 76% of FDA's domestically-grown strawberry samples contained detectable pesticide residues.

SWEET POTATOES

Over one-third of all fresh sweet potatoes analyzed were found to contain residues of one or more pesticides. Seventeen different pesticides were detected in sweet potatoes. The EPA has registered more than 40 different pesticides for use on sweet potatoes and only half of these chemicals can be routinely detected by FDA. Dicloran residues were detected in one-third of all samples. Here are the five pesticides detected most frequently (in order of decreasing occurrence) in fresh sweet potatoes:

Pesticide	Health effects
Dicloran *DCNA, Botran*	No observed reproductive toxicity in one animal study. According to EPA, has not been sufficiently tested for carcinogenicity, birth defects, or mutagenic effects.
Phosmet *Imidan*	Possible human carcinogen. Some evidence of mutagenic effects in laboratory test systems and humans (pesticide factory workers). No observed birth defects or reproductive toxicity in animal studies.
DDT	Probable human carcinogen. Some evidence of reproductive toxicity and adverse liver effects in animal studies. EPA cancelled all uses in the U.S. in 1972 due to carcinogenicity, bioaccumulation, and other chronic effects.
Dieldrin	Probable human carcinogen. Causes birth defects and reproductive toxicity in animal studies. Low levels cause adverse effects on learning capabilities in monkeys. EPA cancelled all uses in the U.S. in 1974 due to carcinogenicity, bioaccumulation, and other chronic effects.
BHC *HCH, 666,* *Hexachlor*	Causes cancer in test animals. Some evidence of male reproductive toxicity in test animals. EPA cancelled all uses in U.S. in 1978 due to carcinogenicity. Residues persist in the environment.

Can residue be reduced by washing?	Residue reduction
YES	Residues remain on surface following foliar treatment, but are absorbed and translocated to edible tissue following soil treatment. Incorporation of dicloran into wax formulations reduces the effectiveness of washing. Washing, peeling, cooking, or heat processing may reduce residues.
YES	Residues remain primarily on the produce surface. Washing or cooking will reduce residues.
YES	Residues remain primarily on the produce surface, although residues may be absorbed into the peel. Washing and peeling reduce residues in root crops, but cooking won't reduce residues once they have been absorbed into the plant tissue.
UNKNOWN	Residues remain primarily on the produce surface, although there is some evidence that residues are systemic in root crops. No information on removal with water. Peeling or cooking may reduce residues.
UNKNOWN	Residues remain primarily on the produce surface, although there is some evidence that residues are systemic in root crops. No information on removal with water.

Waxed produce

You may have already noticed that most of the cucumbers in your supermarket have been waxed. Many other types of fresh produce can also carry thin wax coatings that are not so obvious, including apples, avocados, bell peppers, cantaloupes, cucumbers, eggplants, grapefruits, lemons, limes, melons, oranges, parsnips, passion fruits, peaches, pineapples, pumpkins, rutabagas, squashes, sweet potatoes, tomatoes, and turnips. The FDA has approved half a dozen waxes for use on 18 types of fresh produce. The waxes are composed of shellacs, paraffins, palm oil derivatives, or synthetic resins—ingredients that are also found in some floor and car waxes.

The waxes are used to maintain the cosmetic appeal of food by preventing unsightly shriveling that occurs during natural moisture loss after harvest. These waxes cannot be washed off, and they can seal pesticide residues into the food. Fungicides also can be added to the waxes including benomyl, thiabendazole, ortho-phenylphenol, sodium ortho-phenyl phenate, imazalil, and dicloran.

The Federal Food Drug and Cosmetic Act requires all retail outlets to post prominent signs or labels notifying customers of the presence of waxes. But FDA admits that enforcement of the labeling or sign posting on waxed produce is a low priority. Furthermore, the federal law requires that any pesticides applied to produce after the harvest must be labeled on the shipping container. Retailers, however, are not required to (nor are they prohibited from) identifying these post-harvest pesticides to customers. If these chemicals have been marked on the shipping containers, produce managers—when asked by customers—should be able to identify post-harvest pesticides.

TOMATOES

E very year, Americans on average eat 24 pounds of tomatoes per person. Nearly half of all tomatoes sampled contained residues of one or more pesticides, and 70% of imported tomatoes tested contained residues. Forty-two different pesticides were detected on tomatoes. The laboratory method routinely used by the federal government can detect only 55% of the more than 100 pesticides that can be used on tomatoes. Methamidophos and chlorpyrifos residues were detected on 27% and 19% of the tomato samples respectively. Here are the five pesticides detected most frequently (in order of decreasing occurrence) in fresh tomatoes:

Pesticide	Health effects
Methamidophos *Monitor*	No observed birth defects in one animal study. EPA is reviewing studies submitted to fill previous data gaps for carcinogenicity, birth defects, reproductive toxicity and mutagenic effects.
Chlorpyrifos *Dursban*	No observed carcinogenicity, birth defects or mutagenic effects in available studies. According to EPA, has not been sufficiently tested for chronic toxicity, carcinogenicity, or mutagenic effects.
Chlorothalonil *Bravo*	Probable human carcinogen. Some evidence of chronic health effects including kidney, thyroid, stomach and liver changes, and mutagenic effects in laboratory studies. No observed birth defects in animal studies. Hexachlorobenzene contaminant is a probable human carcinogen and is found in food.
Permethrin *Ambush,* *Pounce*	Possible human carcinogen. Some evidence of reproductive toxicity in one animal study. No observed birth defects or mutagenic effects in laboratory studies.
Dimethoate *Cygon, Rogon*	Some evidence of carcinogenicity, birth defects, reproductive toxicity and mutagenic effects in laboratory studies.

Can residue be reduced by washing?	Residue reduction
NO	Residues are systemic and probably cannot be removed with washing.
UNKNOWN	Residues remain primarily on the produce surface. No information on removal with water. Dried fruits showed higher levels of residues than on fresh fruits because of the concentration effect of dehydration.
YES	Residues remain primarily on the produce surface; however, chlorothalonil metabolites may be systemic. Washing or cooking reduces residues.
YES	Residues remain primarily on the produce surface. Washing with detergent will reduce residues; plain water may not. Processing tomatoes causes residues to concentrate at far greater levels than in fresh produce.
UNKNOWN	Residues are systemic. However, washing, peeling, cooking, or heat processing reduced residues in various studies.

Imported tomatoes

Over three billion pounds of tomatoes were imported into the United States from 1983 to 1985. Tomatoes were imported into the United States from 52 different countries during this three-year period and from 30 countries in each of the three years. Tomatoes from 17 of these countries were not sampled in any of the three years. Imports accounted for 80% of the samples analyzed by FDA and 70% of these had residues.

Domestic tomatoes

California produces 28% of the fresh tomatoes and 86% of the tomatoes grown for processing in the United States. Florida supplies 47% of the fresh tomatoes grown in the United States. In contrast to the frequency of imported tomatoes with pesticide residues, only 23% of the domestically grown tomatoes analyzed by FDA had detectable pesticide residues.

WATER-MELON

O nly four percent of the watermelons sampled were found to contain pesticide residues. Seven different pesticides were detected in watermelons. The EPA has registered approximately 30 different pesticides for use on watermelons, and about 50% of these can be routinely detected by FDA. Aldicarb residues result from illegal use in California and Arizona in 1985. Here are the five pesticides detected most frequently (in order of decreasing occurrence) in fresh watermelon:

Pesticide	Health effects
Methamidophos *Monitor*	No observed birth defects in one animal study. EPA is reviewing studies submitted to fill previous data gaps for carcinogenicity, birth defects, reproductive toxicity and mutagenic effects.
Chlorothalonil *Bravo*	Probable human carcinogen. Some evidence of chronic health effects including kidney, thyroid, stomach and liver changes, and mutagenic effects in laboratory studies. No observed birth defects in animal studies. Hexachlorobenzene contaminant is a probable human carcinogen and is found in food.
Dimethoate *Cygon, Rogon*	Some evidence of carcinogenicity, birth defects, reproductive toxicity and mutagenic effects in laboratory studies.
Carbaryl *Sevin*	Some evidence of adverse kidney effects in humans, and mutagenic effects in laboratory test systems. No observed carcinogenicity or reproductive toxicity in animal studies.
Captan *Merpan,* *Orthocide*	Probable human carcinogen. Some evidence of mutagenic effects in laboratory test systems. EPA initiated Special Review in 1980 due to carcinogenicity, mutagenic effects, and presence of residues in food.

Can residue be reduced by washing?	Residue reduction
NO	Residues are systemic and probably cannot be removed with washing.
YES	Residues remain primarily on the produce surface; however, chlorothalonil metabolites may be systemic. Washing reduces residues.
UNKNOWN	Residues are systemic. However, washing and peeling reduced residues in various studies.
YES	Residues remain primarily on the produce surface. Washing and peeling will reduce residues.
YES	Residues remain primarily on the produce surface. However, the metabolite THPI, a suspected carcinogen, may be systemic. Washing, cooking, or heat processing will reduce residues.

The aldicarb story

Aldicarb was the most frequently detected pesticide in watermelons in 1985, even though use of the chemical on this fruit is illegal. Intensive California and FDA sampling uncovered aldicarb in a large number of watermelons. Aldicarb residues are not expected to continue to occur in watermelons, but the incident raised some serious questions about laboratory detection programs. In the summer of 1985 nearly 1000 people in the western United States were poisoned by illegal residues of aldicarb in watermelons. Several growers applied aldicarb to watermelons when the chemical was not registered for use on this commodity. According to a California Department of Health Services investigation of this incident, a similar but smaller poisoning outbreak occurred several years earlier, but the cause went undetected because the laboratory method for aldicarb could not detect the residue occurring in food and causing the human illness. The Department report also suggested that human poisonings may have occurred from levels of residues in watermelons that were undetectable with the laboratory's analytical test.

3 Federal regulation of pesticides: A record of neglect

Responsibility for protecting the public from pesticide residues in food is shared primarily by the EPA and FDA. Under the Federal Insecticide, Fungicide and Rodenticide Act (FIFRA), EPA has the authority to regulate the sale and use of pesticides in the United States. FIFRA requires that all pesticides sold in the United States be licensed, or registered, for use by EPA. To register a pesticide, EPA must determine that the chemical will not cause "unreasonable adverse effects on the environment" or humans. In other words, that the benefits arising from the chemical's use outweigh the risks. The EPA relies almost exclusively on health and safety tests conducted by the pesticide manufacturer when deciding whether to register a pesticide.

If the pesticide is to be used in the production of a food crop or animal feed, the Federal Food, Drug and Cosmetic Act (FFDCA) requires that, in addition to being registered under FIFRA, the pesticide must have a "tolerance," or maximum allowable limit, for pesticide residues, or an exemption from a tolerance. Tolerances are set by EPA for each *individual* crop or food type, including vegetables, fruits, eggs, meat, and processed food, on which the pesticide will be used.

The FDA enforces the tolerances by conducting nationwide monitoring of food for levels of pesticide residues and implements seizure actions for food products in violation of the established tolerances.[33]

In reality this system does not adequately protect consumers. The EPA itself ranked pesticides in food as one of the most serious health and environmental problems. This result confirmed what numerous reports have previously shown. Since the mid-1970s, numerous Congressional and government reports have suggested there are serious inadequacies in the existing programs that regulate pesticides, particularly residues in food. For example, in order for a pesticide to be licensed for use on a food crop, the manufacturer must submit health effects tests to the federal Environmental Protection Agency to assure the safety of the chemical. The EPA uses these data to establish the maximum safe level, or tolerance, for pesticide residues allowed in food. Yet, in many cases, EPA licensed chemicals for use and established tolerances before key health and safety tests were performed, and therefore cannot ensure that consumers are ingesting only safe amounts of pesticide residues. In other cases, tolerances have been based on data that are inadequate, invalid, or even fabricated. In 1976, FDA investigations uncovered a major scandal at Industrial Bio-Test Laboratories (IBT) in Northbrook, Illinois. Most studies conducted by IBT were subsequently found to be inadequate, invalid, or in some cases even fabricated. The registration of over 200 pesticides relied on IBT data to varying degrees.

The EPA has also established tolerances for cancer-causing pesticides, even though most scientists believe there is no level of exposure to a carcinogen that is safe. The federal pesticide law allows EPA to license any pesticide if the benefits of its use are estimated to exceed the risks. Thus, even carcinogens can be applied to our food if the benefits, primarily calculated in terms of value to growers, are considered substantial. But the Delaney clause of the federal food safety law prohibits the use of cancer-causing additives to food, even though no evidence exists to demonstrate that cancer-causing food additives are more dangerous than cancer-causing pesticides.

Another reason that EPA's tolerances may permit unsafe pesticide residues in food is that EPA relies on estimates of average food consumption in calculating acceptable levels of exposure. For example, when setting a tolerance, EPA estimates that the average American eats no more than 7.5 ounces *per year* of avocado, artichokes, zucchini, melons, nectarines, eggplant, mushrooms, or tangerines. These numbers were developed by taking the total United States annual production of the commodity in the late 1960s and dividing this figure by the nation's population. These averages do not account for special dietary patterns of the population. Further, these figures are unrealistic given the substantially increased consumption of fresh fruits and vegetables in the last twenty years.

Children may be even less protected by EPA's tolerances because these levels are calculated on the basis of an average adult's diet. Children are more exposed to pesticide residues because (1) they eat more food per unit of body weight, and (2) they eat more of certain foods that are likely to contain pesticides. For example, the typical toddler on a body weight basis consumes 19 times more non-citrus fruit juice, 13 times more milk, 7 times more apples, and 6 times more fresh bananas than the typical adult woman.[34] However, EPA does not routinely consider infant and child exposure when setting tolerances.

After EPA establishes the tolerance, the Federal Food and Drug Administration (FDA) is responsible for enforcing the residue limit. Any food containing pesticide residues above the tolerance level is illegal and cannot be sold. However, FDA's system for enforcing tolerances is plagued by problems. The routine laboratory methods that FDA uses to identify pesticides can detect only 40 percent of the chemicals applied to our food. In fact, FDA has acknowledged that 40 percent of the pesticides classified as having a moderate to high health hazard cannot be detected by any of the routine methods.[35] For example, FDA has classified a group of four widely used pesticides known as the EBDCs (ethylene bisdithiocarbamates) as a potentially high hazard that warrants continuous monitoring for residues in food. Approximately one-third of the nation's fruit and vegetables are treated with EBDCs. Yet, FDA cannot detect EBDCs or ETU (ethylenethiourea) with their routine laboratory methods. Although a special scan to detect these compounds is available, FDA has only used this test in the most rare instances. In fact, the U.S. General Accounting Office (GAO) first reported inadequate testing for EBDCs in 1975. During a 1987 Congressional investigation, GAO reported that between 1978 and 1987 only 154 domestic food samples were analyzed for EBDCs and not one single sample of imported food was tested.[36]

A recent government report disclosed that FDA's enforcement is weak because FDA laboratories on average took 28 calendar days to complete sample analysis and processing.[37] In other words, in the time FDA took to complete its laboratory work, most food would have been sold and consumed. Therefore, FDA could not take any action to prevent consumption of food with illegal pesticide residues. The study revealed that for 60 percent of the domestic food cases with illegal residues, FDA did not prevent the sale of the food. In no cases did FDA penalize growers. This means that food containing residues violating tolerances was eaten by the public. With imported foods, the enforcement is marginally better: about 45 percent of the foods with illegal residues were consumed because FDA was unable to prevent sale.[38]

Notes

1. Bryan Bashin, "The Freshness Illusion", *Harrowsmith,* January/February 1987.
2. Ken Kizer, California Department of Health Services, Memorandum to Clare Berryhill, California Department of Food and Agriculture, "Request for Reevaluation of Aldicarb (Temik)", February 3, 1986.
3. Cass Peterson, "Heptachlor Find Causes Milk Recall", *Washington Post,* March 11, 1986.
4. "Three Receive Prison Terms in Heptachlor Contaminated Feed Case", *Pesticide and Toxic Chemical News,* July 27, 1987.
5. Food Marketing Institute, *Trends Update: 1987 Consumer Attitudes and the Supermarket,* 1987.
6. National Academy of Sciences, *Regulating Pesticides: The Delaney Paradox,* 1987.
7. EPA, Office of Pesticide Programs, "Pesticide Industry Sales and Usage 1985 Market Estimates", Table 4, September 1986.
8. Phil Shabecoff, "Pesticide Control Finally Tops the EPA's List of Most Pressing Problems", *New York Times,* March 6, 1986.
9. EPA, Office of Pesticide Programs, "Pesticide Industry Sales and Usage 1985 Market Estimates", Table 3, September 1986.
10. Robert S. Murphy, *et al.,* "Selected Pesticide Residues or Metabolites in Blood and Urine Specimens from a General Population Survey", *Environmental Health Perspectives,* 48: 81–86, 1983.
11. EPA, *Agricultural Chemicals in Ground Water Strategic Plan,* June 1987.
12. David Cohen and Gerald Bowes, *Water Quality and Pesticides: A California Risk Assessment Program,* California Water Resources Control Board, December 20, 1984, with February 26, 1985 update.

13. *Ibid.*
14. GAO, *Pesticides: Need to Enhance FDA's Ability to Protect the Public from Illegal Residues,* October 1986.
15. Shelia Hoar, *et al.,* "Agricultural Herbicide Use and Risk of Lymphoma and Soft-Tissue Sarcoma", *Journal of the American Medical Association,* 256:1141–1147, 1986.
16. Aaron Blair, *et al.,* "Leukemia Among Nebraska Farmers: A Death Certificate Study", *American Journal of Epidemiology,* 110:264–273, 1979. Leon Burmeister, *et al.,* "Selected Cancer Mortality and Farm Practices in Iowa", *American Journal of Epidemiology,* 118:72–77, 1983.
17. Ruth Lowengart, *et al.,* "Childhood Leukemia and Parents' Occupational and Home Exposures", *Journal of National Cancer Institute,* 79: 39–46, 1987.
18. Michael Dover and Brian Croft, *Getting Tough: Public Policy and the Management of Pesticide Resistance,* World Resources Institute, p. 7, November 1984.
19. David Pimental, *et al.,* "Benefits and Costs of Pesticide Use in U.S. Food Production", *BioScience,* 28:772–784, December 1978.
20. Gino Marco, *et al.,* Editor, *Silent Spring Revisited,* American Chemical Society, p. 94, 1987.
21. EPA, *Unfinished Business: A Comparative Assessment of Environmental Problems,* February 1987.
22. National Academy of Sciences, *Regulating Pesticides in Food: The Delaney Paradox,* 1987.
23. National Academy of Sciences, *Toxicity Testing: Strategies to Determine Needs and Priorities,* 1984.
24. *EPA Pesticide Regulatory Program Study,* House Committee on Agriculture Subcommittee on Department Operations, Research, and Foreign Agriculture, 97th Cong., 2d. Sess., 1982.
25. GAO, *Pesticides: EPA's Formidable Task to Assess and Regulate Their Risks,* April 1986.
26. Leon Olson, "The Immune System and Pesticides", *Journal of Pesticide Reform,* Summer 1986.
27. GAO, *Pesticides: Need to Enhance FDA's Ability to Protect the Public from Illegal Residues,* October 1986.
28. USDA, *Agricultural Statistics - 1983,* U.S. Government Printing Office, Washington, D.C., Table 205, 1983.
29. William D. Ruckelshaus, Administrator, EPA, Letter to Congressman James J. Florio, November 8, 1983.
30. James Erlichman, *Gluttons for Punishment,* Penguin, p. 135, 1986. "Farming Brief: Does Nature Know Best?", *The Economist,* pp. 70–72, August 22, 1987.
31. Americans for Safe Food, "Consumer Group Honors 'Safe Food Trailblazers' ", Press Release, January 21, 1987.
32. *Ibid.*
33. USDA is responsible for monitoring poultry and certain egg products for pesticide residues and enforcing the relevant tolerances.

34. USDA, "CSFII - Nationwide Food Consumption Survey: Women 19–50 Years and Their Children 1–5 Years, One Day", Report No. 85-1, 1985.
35. GAO, *Pesticides: Need to Enhance FDA's Ability to Protect the Public from Illegal Residues,* October 1986.
36. Testimony of J. Dexter Peach, Assistant Comptroller General, GAO, before the Subcommittee on Oversight and Investigations, Committee on Energy and Commerce, U.S. House of Representatives, April 30, 1987.
37. GAO, *Food and Drug Administration: Laboratory Analysis of Product Samples Needs to be More Timely,* September 1986.
38. GAO, *Pesticides: Need to Enhance FDA's Ability to Protect the Public From Illegal Residues,* October 1986.

Sources on frequency of pesticides in the 26 commodities

Pesticide monitoring data from the federal and California governments was used to identify the pesticides detected most frequently as residues in the individual commodities. Below are the documents that contain the pesticide monitoring data.

California Department of Food and Agriculture, "Pesticide Residue System: Sample Summary Reports", 1982, 1983, 1984, 1985.
Food and Drug Administration, "Listing of Pesticide Data Sequenced By Industry/Product Within Origin and Sample Flag", 1982, 1983, 1984, 1985.

Sources of additional information

Pesticide reform organizations

Here is a brief list of the major organizations working on pesticide and related environmental issues. They may be able to respond to specific questions or provide information on technical, legal, or legislative issues. There are many other organizations actively involved in pesticide issues at the national, state, and local levels.

Americans for Safe Food
1501 Sixteenth Street, NW
Washington, DC 20036
(202) 332-9110
ASF is a coalition of over 40 consumer, environmental, and rural groups whose goal is to convert consumer dismay about health risks in food into progress toward the general availability of contaminant-free food.

National Coalition Against Misuse of Pesticides
530 Seventh Street, SE
Washington, DC 20003
(202) 543-5450
NCAMP is the primary national coalition of all grassroots organizations working on pesticide issues. Most pesticide reform organizations can be reached by contacting NCAMP. Five times a year, NCAMP publishes *Pesticides and You,* a newsletter on pesticide issues across the nation.

Natural Resources Defense Council
90 New Montgomery Street
San Francisco, CA 94105
(415) 777-0220

NRDC is dedicated to the protection of public health and the environment, and has worked extensively on seeking effective control of pesticides.

Northwest Coalition for Alternatives to Pesticides
P.O. Box 1393
Eugene, OR 97440
(503) 344-5044
NCAP, a five-state coalition of citizen groups working on pesticide issues, publishes the quarterly *Journal of Pesticide Reform*, a comprehensive publication on a wide variety of pesticide topics and related concerns.

Pesticides Action Network—North America Regional Center
Pesticide Education Action Project
P.O. Box 610
San Francisco, CA 94101
(415) 771-7327
PAN is an international coalition of environmental, consumer, farmer, and research organizations, voluntary development agencies and individuals who are opposed to the worldwide misuse of poisonous pesticides.

Organizations promoting sustainable agriculture

The majority of organizations involved in sustainable or alternative agriculture are active on the regional or local level. Here are some of the groups with a national focus that can identify the most suitable group in your local area.

Bio-Integral Resource Center
P.O. Box 7414
Berkeley, CA 94707
BIRC specializes in information on least-toxic methods for managing any pests found in homes or gardens. *The Common Sense Pest Control Quarterly* provides up-to-date information about pests found in homes, on pets, and in the garden, and is written for non-technical audiences. A Publications Catalog which lists about 50 publications on individual pests is available for $1.00.

Organic Crop Improvement Association
P.O. Box 729A
White Oak Road
New Holland, PA 17557
OCIA is a farmer-owned international organization which provides information on methods to reduce and eliminate pesticide use and certifies individual farmers that meet OCIA's organic farming standards. If you send a self-addressed stamped envelope, they will send you a list of sources of OCIA-certified organic food in your area.

Organic Food Producers Association of North America
P.O. Box 31
Belchertown, MA 01007

OFPANA is a trade association formed by organic farm associations, food processors, distributors, and supporters to establish and maintain standards of excellence for organic food businesses. OFPANA is a marketing network for high-quality, authentic organic food that should be contacted by supermarkets seeking a supply of organic food.

Rodale Press and Research Center
33 E. Minor Street
Emmaus, PA 18098
(215) 967-5171
The Rodale Center publishes *Organic Gardening, New Farm,* and *Prevention* magazines. The Center also develops, tests, and publicizes new farming techniques that reduce the need for pesticides and chemical fertilizers. If you send a self-addressed stamped envelope to *Organic Gardening*'s Reader Service, they can provide you with free lists of organic farming certification organizations, advice and information groups, a directory of resources on alternative agriculture, and an information packet on organic pest control—all developed for their Regeneration Gardeners Network.

Government agencies

The two primary federal agencies regulating pesticides in food are the Environmental Protection Agency and the Food and Drug Administration. The United States Department of Agriculture administers the Agricultural Extension Service whose county agents advise farmers on agricultural production and pest control. States also play a role in pesticide regulation. Contact your state's departments of agriculture and public health to learn about their specific programs on pesticides.

Lee Thomas, Administrator
Environmental Protection Agency
401 M Street, SW
Washington, DC 20460

John A. Moore, Assistant Administrator
Pesticides and Toxic Substances
Environmental Protection Agency
401 M Street, SW
Washington, DC 20460
The EPA regulates the sale and use of pesticides. EPA decides which pesticides will be registered for use and cancels the use of chemicals that pose unreasonable risks. EPA determines the acceptable level (also called tolerance) of pesticides in food.

Frank E. Young, Commissioner
Food and Drug Administration
Department of Health and Human Services
5600 Fishers Lane
Rockville, MD 20857

The FDA monitors food to ensure that pesticide residue levels do not exceed EPA's acceptable levels, or tolerances. FDA is also charged with seizing food tht violates EPA's tolerances and taking enforcement actions against violators.

U.S. Congress

You can write your senators and representatives to express your views on pesticide issues.

Senator_____
U.S. Senate
Washington, DC 20510

Representative_____
U.S. House of Representatives
Washington, DC 20515

Further reading

Breaking the Pesticide Habit: Alternatives to Twelve Hazardous Pesticides, Terry Gipps, International Alliance for Sustainable Agriculture, 1987. (Available from IASA, University of Minnesota, Newman Center, 1701 University Avenue SE, Minneapolis, MN 55414. $14.95.)
Describes alternatives to the pesticides included in Pesticide Action Network's "Dirty Dozen" campaign. This campaign identified 12 extremely hazardous pesticides that are responsible for most of the pesticide deaths and much of the environmental damage in the developing world.

Circle of Poison: Pesticides and People in a Hungry World, David Weir and Mark Schapiro, Institute for Food and Development Policy, 1981. (Available from IFDP, 145 Ninth St., San Francisco, CA 94103. $3.95.)
Documents the international sales of the most deadly pesticides and tells how they return to the United States via imported food.

Food and Drug Administration: Laboratory Analysis of Product Samples Needs to be More Timely, GAO, September 1986.
Pesticides: Better Sampling and Enforcement Needed on Imported Food, GAO, September 1986.
Pesticides: EPA's Formidable Task to Assess and Regulate Their Risks, GAO, April 1986.
Pesticides: Need to Enhance FDA's Ability to Protect the Public From Illegal Residues, GAO, October 1986. (Available from U.S. General Accounting Office, P.O. Box 6015, Gaithersburg, MD 20877. Free.)
Audits of the adequacy of most aspects of the federal government's program to regulate pesticides in food.

Guess What's Coming to Dinner: Contaminants in our Food, Americans

for Safe Food, 1987. (Available from Center for Science in the Public Interest, 1501 Sixteenth St. NW, Washington, DC 20036. $3.50.)
An overview of many food contamination issues including pesticides, antibiotics, food additives, and PCBs.

Harvest of Unknowns: Pesticide Contamination in Imported Foods, Shelley Hearne, 1984. (Available from NRDC, 122 E. 42nd St., New York, NY 10168. $7.50.)
A discussion of the unique problems posed by pesticides in imported food.

The Health Detective's Handbook: A Guide to the Investigation of Environmental Health Hazards by Nonprofessionals, M. Legator, B. Harper and M. Scott, 1985. (Available from The Johns Hopkins University Press, 701 W. 40th St., Baltimore, MD 21211.)
A thorough guide for citizens to evaluate whether adverse health effects in their community may be related to toxic substances.

Healthy Harvest II: A Directory of Sustainable Agriculture and Horticulture Organizations, S.J. Sanzone, J. Burman and M.A. Hage, eds., 1987–88. (Available from Potomac Valley Press, 1424 16th St. NW, Suite 105, Washington, DC 20036. $10.95.)
Provides descriptions of the activities and publications of agricultural, research, and political organizations.

On the Trail of A Pesticide: A Guide to Learning About the Chemistry, Effects and Testing of Pesticides, Mary O'Brien, Northwest Coalition for Alternatives to Pesticides, 1984. (Available from NCAP, P.O. Box 1393, Eugene, OR 97440. $14.00.)
An exhaustive primer for citizen activists on pesticides, including discussions of toxicology and environmental effects.

The Organic Network, Jean Winter, 1984. (Available from Eden Acres, Inc., 12100 Lima Center Road, Clinton, MI 49236. $15.00.)
The directory lists organic growers and buyers, and individuals, farmers, and businesses that sell organically grown foods, including produce, milk, eggs and meats mainly in the U.S.

Organic Wholesalers Directory and Yearbook, California Agrarian Action Project, 1987. (Available from CAAP, P.O. Box 464, Davis, CA 95617. $19.00 plus $1.75 shipping and handling. California residents add 6% sales tax.)
An annual guide for farmers who want to sell their organic commodities through a wholesaler and for retailers looking for wholesale markets for quality, organic food. Although most of the information comes from California, this would be a very useful tool for supermarket produce managers nationwide.

Pesticides: A Community Action Guide, CONCERN, November 1987. (Available from CONCERN, Inc., 1794 Columbia Road NW, Washington, DC 20009. $3.00.)
An informative overview of pesticide issues.

The Pesticide Handbook: Profiles for Action, International Organization of Consumers Unions, Second Edition, 1986. (Available from International Organization of Consumers Unions, P.O. Box 1045, 10830 Penang, Malaysia.)

A description of the health effects of over 40 pesticides commonly used worldwide, and useful sources of information on international pesticide issues.

Pesticides in Food: What the Public Needs to Know, Lawrie Mott and Martha Broad, 1984.

Pesticide Reregistration: An Evaluation of EPA's Progress, Lawrie Mott, 1986. (Available from NRDC, 90 New Montgomery St., San Francisco, CA 94105. $12.50 first class mail, $10.00 book rate.)

A 1984 analysis of the hazards posed by pesticides in food with recommendations for reform. A 1986 study of EPA's efforts to reevaluate the safety of older, inadequately tested pesticides.

Regulating Pesticides in Food: The Delaney Paradox, National Academy of Sciences, 1987. (Available from National Academy Press, 2101 Constitution Avenue NW, Washington, DC 20418. $19.95.)

A lengthy report on the potential risks posed by pesticides in food and different statutory approaches for regulating pesticides in food.

Silent Spring, Rachel Carson, Houghton Mifflin, Boston, 1962. (Available from Penguin Books, 625 Madison Avenue, New York, NY 10022.)

An articulate, readable, and still timely description of the problems posed by pesticides.

Glossary

Active ingredient. The substance in a pesticide product designed to kill or control the target organism. Other ingredients in pesticide products, called "inerts," do not affect the target organism.

Acute toxicity. The toxic reaction that usually occurs shortly after exposure to a toxic agent (*e.g.,* a few hours or days).

Cancer. The unregulated overgrowth of cells. In medical terminology, a cancer is a malignant tumor.

Carbamates. A class of synthetic organic pesticides that are used as insecticides, fungicides, or nematicides. They have similar effects on nerve function as organophosphates.

Carcinogen. A substance that can produce cancer (malignant tumors) in experimental animals or is known to do so in humans.

Chronic toxicity. The toxic effects such as cancer, reproductive toxicity, or birth defects that usually occur weeks, months, or years after exposure to a toxic agent, or as a result of long-term, low-level exposure.

Dose level. The amount of chemical administered to a test animal or organism, often described in terms of milligrams per kilogram of body weight or parts per million.

Epidemiology. The study in human populations of the incidence and distribution of disease or toxicity.

Foliar application. The application of a chemical preparation to the leaves or foliage of plants.

Formulation. A pesticide formulation is sometimes called a pesticide product. Few pesticide active ingredients are sold commercially without being mixed with other ingredients—carriers, diluents, solvents, wetting agents, or emulsifiers.

Fumigant. A substance or mixture of substances which produce gas, vapor, fume or smoke intended to destroy insects, bacteria, or rodents. Fumigants may be volatile liquids and solids as well as substances already gaseous. They may be used to disinfest the interiors of buildings, or the soil.

Fungicides. Chemicals used to kill or suppress the growth of all fungi or a certain fungus.

Genetic mutation. An alteration in genetic material which is passed on from one generation to the next.

Herbicides. Chemicals used to kill or suppress the growth of all or a certain type of plant.

Illegal residue. The presence of an active ingredient in amounts above the tolerance on a crop at harvest. In some cases, any amount of chemical present on the crop is considered illegal if no tolerance exists for the pesticide on the commodity.

Immunotoxicology. The study of the effects of chemicals and environmental contaminants on immune systems of animals and humans. Immune system effects can include increased infections, allergic reactions, cancers, and autoimmune diseases.

Inert ingredient. A substance contained in a pesticide product or formulation that is not intended to kill or control the target pest. Materials include solvents, emulsifiers, wetting agents, carriers, diluents, and conditioning agents.

Insecticides. Chemicals used to kill a wide variety or a specific type of insect.

Integrated pest management. The use of two or more methods to control or prevent damage by a pest or pests. These include cultural practices, use of biological control agents, and can even include the use of selective pesticides.

Metabolites. A compound derived, in the case of a pesticide, by chemical, biological, or physical action upon the pesticide within a living organism (plant, insect, or higher animal). The metabolite may be more, equally or less toxic than the original compound. Metabolites can also be produced by the action of environmental factors such as temperature or sunlight.

Mutagen. A substance or agent that produces genetic changes in living cells.

Nematodes. Tiny wormlike organisms that inhabit soil.

Neurotoxicity. The state of toxic effects on the nervous system. Severe neurotoxic effects can include visual problems, muscle twitching and weakness, and abnormalities of brain function and behavior.

Oncogenicity. The tendency for the development of tumors (malignant or benign) in organisms exposed to a chemical substance.

Organochlorines. A class of chemical compounds produced by the addition of chlorine atoms to hydrocarbons. Many of them (*e.g.,* DDT, dieldrin, and endrin) had insecticidal properties and became the most successful of the early synthetic insecticides. These insecticides are characterized by their persistence in the environment.

Organophosphates. A class of pesticides containing phosphorus that are used primarily as insecticides by disrupting nerve function.

Persistent pesticides. Pesticides that remain in the environment and do not degrade or metabolize to innocuous constituents for months or perhaps years.

Plant growth regulator. A preparation which alters the behavior of plants or the produce thereof through physiological (hormonal), rather than physical, action. It may act to accelerate or retard growth, prolong or break a dormant condition, or promote rooting.

Potency. A measure of the relative strength of a chemical.

Pyrethroids. Synthetic organic insecticides that mimic the structure and activity of pyrethrum, a natural insecticide produced by plants.

Reentry interval. The period of time immediately following the application of a pesticide to a field when unprotected workers should not enter.

Residue. That quantity of a substance, especially of pesticide active ingredient, remaining on or in a surface or crop (including livestock products).

Rodenticide. A preparation intended for the control of rodents (rats or mice) and related animals, such as gophers.

Special review. A regulatory procedure adopted by the U.S. EPA to rapidly review the hazards of a pesticide in order to decide whether the chemical should remain in use and whether any restrictions should be placed on its use. A chemical is placed into special review, formerly called Rebuttable Presumption Against Registration (RPAR), when its risks exceed certain criteria EPA has established, such as causing cancer or environmental harm.

Synergism. The tendency of chemicals acting in combination to produce effects greater than the sum of the effects of the individual chemicals.

Systemic pesticides. Pesticides that are translocated to other parts of a plant or animal than those to which the material is applied.

Teratogenicity. The tendency for the formation of birth defects in the offspring of pregnant organisms exposed to a chemical substance.

Tolerance. The maximum amount of pesticide residue that is legally permitted in a food. EPA sets a distinct residue limit for each individual food to which the pesticide may be applied.

Toxicity. The harmful effects produced by a chemical.

Translocation. The distribution of a pesticide chemical from the point of absorption (plant leaves, stems, sometimes roots) to other points. Translocation occurs also in animals treated with certain pesticides.

Bibliography

Sources on toxicology of individual pesticides

The materials used to identify the health effects of the pesticides included in this book are presented below. First the sources used as general references are given. Then the references for specific chemicals are presented.

General sources

California Assembly Office of Research, *The Leaching Fields: A Nonpoint Threat to Groundwater,* March 1985.

Douglas Campt, Office of Pesticide Programs, EPA, Letter to Karen Snyder, NRDC, July 14, 1987.

J. Doull, C.D. Klaassen, and M.O. Amdur, *Casarett and Doull's Toxicology: The Basic Science of Poisons,* Third Edition, Macmillan Publishing Company, 1986.

EPA, Office of Pesticide Programs, *Report on the Status of Chemicals in the Special Review Program, Registration Standards Program, and Data Call-In Program,* September 1986.

Farm Chemicals Handbook 1987, Meister Publishing Company, Willoughby, Ohio, 1987.

John A. Moore, EPA, Letter to Congressman Henry Waxman, Committee on Energy and Commerce, House of Representatives, October 2, 1985.

National Academy of Sciences, *Regulating Pesticides in Food: The Delaney Paradox,* 1987.

Marshall Sittig, *Handbook of Toxic and Hazardous Chemicals,* Noyes Publications, 1981.

Sidney Weinstein, *Fruits of Your Labor: A Guide to Pesticide Hazards for California Field Workers,* Labor Occupational Health Program, University of California, Berkeley, 1984.

Acephate

California Department of Food and Agriculture (CDFA), "SB 950 Tox Summary", October 1, 1986, revised February 5, 1987.

EPA, *Acephate Draft Registration Standard,* September 1985.

Aldicarb

CDFA, "SB 950 Tox Summary", February 10, 1987.

EPA, "Aldicarb Fact Sheet", March 30, 1984.

M.C. Fiore, *et al.,* "Chronic Exposure to Aldicarb Contaminated Groundwater and Human Immune Function", Wisconsin Department of Public Health, September 3, 1986.

Ken Kizer, California Department of Health Services (DOHS), Memorandum to Clare Berryhill, CDFA, "Request for Reevaluation of Aldicarb (Temik)", February 3, 1986.

Azinphos-methyl

EPA, "Azinphos-methyl Fact Sheet", September 30, 1986.

EPA, "O,O-Dimethyl S-[(4-oxo-1,2,3-benzotriazin-3(4H)-yl)methyl] phosphorodithioate: Proposed Tolerances", 45 Federal Register 63888, September 26, 1980.

BHC

EPA, "Benzene Hexachloride: Proposed Revocation of Food Additive Regulation", 50 Federal Register 120, January 2, 1985.

Captan

CDFA, "SB 950 Tox Summary", November 6, 1986, revised May 5, 1987.

EPA, "Captan Fact Sheet", March 6, 1986.

Carbaryl

EPA, *Carbaryl Decision Document,* December 1980.

EPA, "Carbaryl Fact Sheet", March 30, 1984.

EPA, "Carbaryl: Pesticide Tolerances", 51 Federal Register 15353, April 23, 1986.

Mary H. O'Brien, "Carbaryl", prepared for *Forest Watch,* Northwest Coalition for Alternatives to Pesticides, June 29, 1986.

Warren Schultz, "The Trouble with Carbaryl", *Organic Gardening,* October 1984.

Chlordane

Diane Baxter, "Chlordane: A Pesticide Review—Health and Environmental Effects and Alternatives", National Coalition Against the Misuse of Pesticides (NCAMP), 1986.

CDFA, "Draft Policy of the Health and Safety Unit of the Division of Pest Management Concerning Requests for Registration of Products Containing Chlordane to be used as a Termiticide by Householders", September 20, 1983.

CDFA, "SB 950 Tox Summary", January 14, 1987.

EPA, "Chlordane Fact Sheet", January 1987.

EPA, "Chlordane: Revocation of Tolerance", 50 Federal Register 23717, June 5, 1985.

EPA, Office of Drinking Water, "Chlordane Health Advisory", September 30, 1985.

International Organization of Consumers Unions, *The Pesticide Handbook: Profiles for Action,* Penang, Malaysia, 1986.

NCAMP, "Chlordane Fact Sheet", 1986.

John T. Schneller, "Persistent Poison", *Columbia Daily Tribune,* p. 63, February 16, 1983.

Chlorobenzilate

EPA, "Chlorobenzilate Fact Sheet", 1984.

EPA, "Ethyl 4,4'-Dichlorobenzilate: Revocation of Tolerances", 50 Federal Register 23720, June 5, 1985.

Chlorothalonil

CDFA, "SB 950 Tox Summary", June 23, 1987.

EPA, "Chlorothalonil: Pesticide Tolerance", 50 Federal Register 26592, June 27, 1985.

EPA, "Chlorothalonil Fact Sheet", CFS/RS-84-13, September 1984.

EPA, *Chlorothalonil Registration Standard,* September 1984.

Chlorpropham (CIPC)

CDFA, "SB 950 Tox Summary", April 25, 1986.

EPA, "Tox One-Liners - 510A CIPC", File last updated January 14, 1985, Release July 9, 1986.

J.J. Jacobson, Sierra Club, Letter to Lawrie Mott, NRDC, September 5, 1986.

Tobi Jones, CDFA, Phone Conversation with Karen Snyder, NRDC, October 15, 1986.

Chlorpyrifos

CDFA, "SB 950 Tox Summary", August 11, 1986, revised June 5, 1987.

EPA, "Chlorpyrifos: Pesticide Tolerance", 50 Federal Register 21876, May 29, 1985.

EPA, "Chlorpyrifos Fact Sheet", 1984.

EPA, *Chlorpyrifos Registration Standard,* September 28, 1984.

NCAMP, "Chlorpyrifos", *Pesticides and You,* June 1986.

Cyhexatin

CDFA, "CDFA Suspends Registration of Pesticide Plictran", Press Release No. 87-104, June 24, 1987.

CDFA, "SB 950 Tox Summary", August 6, 1986, revised November 24, 1986, January 29, 1987, and May 27, 1987.

EPA, "Cyhexatin Fact Sheet", June 30, 1985.
EPA, *Cyhexatin Registration Standard,* June 1985.

DCPA

CDFA, "SB 950 Tox Summary" (Chlorthal-dimethyl), May 8, 1987.
EPA, "Dimethyl Tetrachloroterephthalate: Proposed Tolerances", 49 Federal Register 21768, May 23, 1984.
FDA, *Surveillance Index,* Supplement No. 10, June 5, 1985.

DDT

EPA, "DDT and TDE: Proposed Revocation of Food and Feed Additive Regulations", 50 Federal Register 10070, March 13, 1985.
Pesticide Action Network, "The 'Dirty Dozen' Information Packet", Pesticide Education and Action Project, San Francisco, California, 1985.

Demeton

CDFA, "SB 950 Tox Summary", July 15, 1986.
EPA, "Demeton Fact Sheet", February 27, 1985.

Diazinon

CDFA, "SB 950 Tox Summary", July 29, 1986.
EPA, "Diazinon Data Call-In Notice", February 18, 1983.
EPA, "Diazinon Fact Sheet", September 1986.
EPA, "O,O-Diethyl O-(2-isopropyl-6-methyl-4-pyrimidinyl) phosphorothioate: Proposed Tolerance", 49 Federal Register 42752, October 24, 1984.
K.T. Maddy, W.G. Cusick, and S. Edmiston, "Degradation of Dislodgeable Residues of Chlorpyrifos and Diazinon on Turf: A Preliminary Study", Worker Health and Safety Unit, CDFA, HS-1196, July 10, 1984.
Joan M. Spyker and David L. Avery, "Neurobehavioral Effects of Prenatal Exposure to the Organophosphate Diazinon in Mice", *Journal of Toxicology and Environmental Health,* 3:989-1002, 1977.

Dicloran

EPA, "Dicloran Fact Sheet", January 9, 1984.

Dieldrin

EPA, "Aldrin and Dieldrin: Proposed Revocation of Tolerances", 50 Federal Register 10080, March 13, 1985.

Dimethoate

EPA, *Dimethoate Registration Standard,* March 1983.
EPA, "Dimethoate: Proposed Tolerances", 48 Federal Register 52951, November 23, 1983.

FDA, *Surveillance Index,* revised January 15, 1980.

Tobi Jones, CDFA, Phone Conversation with Karen Snyder, NRDC, October 15, 1986.

National Institute for Occupational Safety and Health, *Registry of Toxic Effects of Chemical Substances,* 1981–1982 edition, U.S. Department of Health and Human Services, June 1983.

Diphenylamine

EPA, *Daminozide Special Review Position Document 2/3/4: Draft,* September 12, 1985.

EPA, "Tox One – Liners-398 Diphenylamine", File last updated July 23, 1984, Release November 13, 1986.

FDA, *Surveillance Index,* September 16, 1983.

Tobi Jones, CDFA, Phone Conversation with Karen Snyder, NRDC, October 15, 1986.

Endosulfan

CDFA, "Notice of Initial Decisions Concerning Reevaluation of Pesticide Products - Endosulfan", October 21, 1985.

CDFA, "SB 950 Tox Summary", November 14, 1986.

EPA, "Endosulfan: Proposed Tolerance", 48 Federal Register 24394, June 1, 1983.

EPA, *Endosulfan Registration Standard,* April 1982.

Ethion

EPA, *Ethion Registration Standard,* December 23, 1982.

Fenvalerate

CDFA, "SB 950 Tox Summary", January 27, 1987.

EPA, "Cyano-(3-phenoxyphenyl) methyl-4-chloro-alpha-(1-methylethyl) benzene acetate: Pesticide Tolerance", 50 Federal Register 31893, August 7, 1985.

EPA, "Cyano-(3-phenoxyphenyl) methyl-4-chloro-alpha-(1-methylethyl) benzene acetate: Pesticide Tolerances", 51 Federal Register 43643, December 3, 1986.

Iprodione

CDFA, "SB 950 Tox Summary", November 26, 1986, revised July 9, 1987.

EPA, "Iprodione: Pesticide Tolerances", 51 Federal Register 6739, February 26, 1986.

EPA, "Iprodione: Pesticide Tolerances", 52 Federal Register 4356, February 11, 1987.

Lindane

CDFA, "SB 950 Tox Summary", December 11, 1986.

EPA, "Lindane Fact Sheet", September 30, 1985.

"U.S. Dropping Pesticide Ban", *New York Times,* October 14, 1983.

Malathion

M. Balter, "Malathion's 'Safety' May Be Overstated", *Los Angeles Times,* March 18, 1985.

Citizens for a Better Environment, "Testimony of Steve Dreistadt before the Medfly Health Advisory Committee's Public Hearing on Health Impacts of Medfly Eradication in San Jose, California", December 2, 1981.

CDFA, "SB 950 Tox Summary", July 30, 1986, revised February 23, 1987.

EPA, "Malathion: Proposed Tolerance", 47 Federal Register 50933, November 10, 1982.

J. Nesmith, "Pathologist Finds Career Is Ruined: Cancer Expert Loses Job After Paper On Malathion", *Oakland Tribune,* August 29, 1984.

Methamidophos

EPA, *Methamidophos Registration Standard,* September 30, 1982.

EPA, "Methamidophos: Proposed Tolerance", 48 Federal Register 39473, August 31, 1983.

Methidathion

CDFA, "SB 950 Tox Summary", November 21, 1986.

EPA, *Methidathion Registration Standard,* January 13, 1983.

EPA, "Methidathion: Proposed Tolerance", 45 Federal Register 85103, December 24, 1980.

Methomyl

CDFA, "SB 950 Tox Summary", August 8, 1986.

EPA, *Methomyl Registration Standard,* October 1981.

EPA, "Methomyl: Proposed Tolerances", 47 Federal Register 16050, April 14, 1982.

Methyl Parathion

CDFA, "Update on the Status of Reevaluations", presented at Pesticide Registration and Evaluation Committee Meeting, September 19, 1986.

CDFA, "SB 950 Tox Summary", November 3, 1986.

EPA, "Methyl Parathion Fact Sheet", December 1986.

EPA, "Methyl Parathion: Proposed Tolerances", 49 Federal Register 29110, July 18, 1984.

Mevinphos

CDFA, "SB 950 Tox Summary", May 28, 1987.

EPA, "Methyl 3-[(dimethoxyphosphinyl)oxy] butenoate, Alpha and Beta Isomers: Proposed Tolerance", 49 Federal Register 42754, October 24, 1984.

Parathion

CDFA, "Update on the Status of Reevaluations", presented at Pesticide Registration and Evaluation Committee Meeting, September 19, 1986.

CDFA, "SB 950 Tox Summary", November 4, 1986, revised February 26, 1987.

EPA, "Parathion Data Call-In Notice", November 4, 1981.

EPA, "Parathion Fact Sheet", December 1986.

Permethrin

E. Budd, *et al.,* "Permethrin: Assessment of Chronic and Oncogenic Effects, A Summary", Hazard Evaluation Division, EPA, April 5, 1982.

CDFA, "SB 950 Tox Summary", January 9, 1987.

EPA, "Permethrin—Tolerances and Exemption from Tolerances for Pesticide Chemicals in or on Raw Agricultural Commodities", (October 13, 1982 - to be published).

EPA, "Permethrin: Pesticide Tolerances", 51 Federal Register 12885, April 16, 1986.

Adrian Gross, EPA, Memorandum to John Melone, EPA, "Summary of Chronic and Oncogenic Effects of Permethrin", May 7, 1982.

Phosmet

CDFA, "SB 950 Tox Summary", October 28, 1986, revised February 11, 1987.

EPA, "N-(Mercaptomethyl) phthalimide S-(O,O-dimethyl phosphorodithioate): Proposed Tolerance", 48 Federal Register 22337, May 18, 1983.

EPA, "Phosmet Fact Sheet", October 1, 1986.

Sulfallate

EPA, "2-Chloroallyldiethyldithiocarbamate: Proposed Tolerances", 46 Federal Register 27973, May 22, 1981.

FDA, *Surveillance Index,* October 21, 1985.

Thiabendazole

EPA, "Thiabendazole: Proposed Tolerance", 47 Federal Register 654, January 6, 1982.

Eero Ruuttila, *After the Harvest: Assessing the Risks of Storage and Shelf Life Pesticides,* 1986.

Trifluralin

CDFA, "SB 950 Tox Summary", May 27, 1987.

EPA, *Trifluralin Position Document 4 (Treflan),* July 1982.

EPA, "Trifluralin: Proposed Tolerance", 47 Federal Register 6033, February 10, 1982.

EPA, *Trifluralin Registration Standard,* August 1986.

Vinclozolin

CDFA, "SB 950 Tox Summary", July 30, 1986.

EPA, "Pesticide Tolerance for 3-(3,5-Dichlorophenyl)-5-ethenyl 5-methyl-2, 4-oxazolidinedione", 51 Federal Register 3635, January 29, 1986.

Sources on removal of pesticide residues

The materials used to determine whether residues of the pesticides included in this book could be removed by water washing are presented below. First the sources used as general references are given. Then the references for specific chemicals are presented.

General sources

The British Crop Protection Council, *The Pesticide Manual: A World Compendium,* Charles R. Worthing, ed., Seventh Edition, 1983.

Food and Agriculture Organization of the United Nations, *Pesticide Residues in Food-1983: Report of the Joint Meeting of the FAO Panel of Experts on Pesticide Residues in Food and the Environment and the WHO Expert Group on Pesticide Residues,* FAO Plant Production and Protection Paper No. 56, 1984 and Paper No. 78, 1986.

Acephate

EPA, *Acephate Draft Registration Standard,* September 1985.

FDA, *Surveillance Index,* April 25, 1980.

Technical Assessment Systems, Inc., *Pesticides in Our Food: Facts, Issues, Debates, and Perceptions,* May 18, 1987.

Aldicarb

FDA, *Surveillance Index,* May 2, 1980.

Ken Kizer, DOHS, Memorandum to Clare Berryhill, CDFA, "Request for Reevaluation of Aldicarb (Temik)", February 3, 1986.

Azinphos-methyl

R.F. Albach and B.J. Lime, "Pesticide Residue Reduction by the Process of Preparing Whole Orange Puree", *Journal of Agricultural and Food Chemistry,* 24:1217–1220, 1976.

EPA, "Azinphos-Methyl Fact Sheet", September 30, 1986.

FDA, *Surveillance Index,* June 18, 1981.

C. Russo, C.M. Lanza, *et al.,* "Decay of Phosphorylated Insecticides on Sanguinello Moscato Oranges", (abstract), *Essenze Derivati Agrumari,* 53(1), 1983.

BHC

EPA, "Benzene Hexachloride: Proposed Revocation of Tolerances", 50 Federal Register 125, January 2, 1985.

FDA, *Surveillance Index,* November 4, 1979.

Captan

EPA, "Captan Fact Sheet", March 6, 1986.

FDA, *Surveillance Index,* April 4, 1980.

R. Frank, J. Northover, and H.E. Braun, "Persistence of Captan on Apples, Grapes, and Pears in Ontario, Canada 1981–1983", *Journal of Agricultural and Food Chemistry,* 33:514–518, 1985.

R. Frank, H.E. Braun, and J. Stanek, "Removal of Captan from Treated Apples", *Archives of Environmental Contamination and Toxicology,* 12:265–269, 1983.

Dalia M. Gilvydis, *et al.,* "Residues of Captan and Folpet in Strawberries and Grapes", *Journal of the Association of Official Analytical Chemists,* 69:803–806, 1986.

G. Melkebeke, *et al.,* "Effects of Some Culinary Treatments on Residue Contents of Spinach", (abstract), *Revue de l'Agriculture,* 2:36, 1983.

Carbaryl

EPA, "Carbaryl Fact Sheet", March 30, 1984.

FDA, *Surveillance Index,* May 7, 1980.

E.R. Elkins, *et al.,* "Removal of DDT, Malathion, and Carbaryl from Green Beans by Commercial and Home Preparative Procedures", *Journal of Agricultural and Food Chemistry,* 16:962–966, 1968.

R.P. Farrow, *et al.,* "Effect of Commercial and Home Preparative Procedures on Parathion and Carbaryl Residues in Broccoli", *Journal of Agricultural and Food Chemistry,* 17:75–79, 1969.

R.P. Farrow, *et al.,* "Removal of DDT, Malathion, and Carbaryl from Tomatoes by Commercial and Home Preparative Methods", *Journal of Agricultural and Food Chemistry,* 16:65–71, 1968.

V.S. Kavadia and B.L. Pareek, "Residues of Phorate, Carbaryl, and Endosulfan in Peas *(Pisum sativum)*", *Journal of Food Science and Technology,* 18(4), 1981.

F.C. Lamb, *et al.,* "Removal of DDT, Parathion, and Carbaryl from Spinach by Commercial and Home Preparative Methods", *Journal of Agricultural and Food Chemistry,* 16:967–973, 1968.

Chlordane

EPA, "Chlordane Fact Sheet", January 1987.

Samuel S. Epstein, *The Politics of Cancer,* Sierra Club Books, 1978.

Chlorobenzilate

R.F. Albach and B.J. Lime, "Pesticide Residue Reduction by the Process of Preparing Whole Orange Puree", *Journal of Agricultural and Food Chemistry,* 24:1217–1220, 1976.

M. Colakoglu and Y. Hisil, "Removal of Dimethoate and Chlorobenzilate Residues during the Processing of Apple Juice", (abstract), *Proceedings of the 6th International Congress of Food Science and Technology,* 1, 1983.

FDA, *Surveillance Index,* November 27, 1979.

Chlorothalonil

EPA, "Chlorothalonil Fact Sheet", September 1984.

FDA, *Surveillance Index,* April 24, 1980.

John A. Moore, Assistant Administrator for Pesticides and Toxic Substances, EPA, Statement before the Committee on Agriculture, Nutrition, and Forestry, U.S. Senate, May 20, 1987.

Chlorpropham (CIPC)

FDA, *Surveillance Index,* August 7, 1980.

Chlorpyrifos

L.G. Adeishvili and E.K. Ordzhonikidze, "Residues of 'Etafos' and Dursban in Citrus Fruits", (abstract), *Khimiya v Sel'skom Khozyaistve,* 21(4), 1983.

EPA, "Chlorpyrifos Fact Sheet", September 1984.

FDA, *Surveillance Index,* July 31, 1980.

G. McDonald, G.A. Buchanan and G.R. Griffiths, "Insecticide Application and Degradation in Sultana Grapes Grown for Drying", *Pesticide Science,* 14:528–536, 1983.

Cyhexatin

EPA, "Cyhexatin Fact Sheet", June 30, 1985.

EPA, *Cyhexatin Registration Standard,* June 1985.

FDA, *Surveillance Index,* April 9, 1980.

A.E. Tatevosyan and D.S. Aleksanyan, "Hygiene Regulation of the Content of Plictran in Food Products", (abstract), *Voprosy Pitaniya,* 5, 1984.

DCPA

FDA, *Surveillance Index,* June 5, 1985.

DDT

E.R. Elkins, *et al.,* "Removal of DDT, Malathion, and Carbaryl from Green Beans by Commercial and Home Preparative Procedures", *Journal of Agricultural and Food Chemistry,* 16:962–966, 1968.

EPA, "DDT and TDE: Proposed Revocation of Tolerances", 50 Federal Register 10077, March 13, 1985.

R.P. Farrow, *et al.,* "Removal of DDT, Malathion, and Carbaryl from Tomatoes by Commercial and Home Preparative Methods", *Journal of Agricultural and Food Chemistry,* 16:65–71, 1968.

F.C. Lamb, *et al.,* "Removal of DDT, Parathion, and Carbaryl from Spinach by Commercial and Home Preparative Methods", *Journal of Agricultural and Food Chemistry,* 16:967–973, 1968.

F.C. Lamb, *et al.,* "Behavior of DDT in Potatoes during Commercial and Home Preparation", *Journal of Agricultural and Food Chemistry,* 16:272–275, 1968.

Demeton

EPA, "Demeton Fact Sheet", February 27, 1985.

FDA, *Surveillance Index,* January 28, 1983.

Diazinon

G. Melkebeke, *et al.,* "Effects of Some Culinary Treatments on Residue Contents of Spinach", (abstract), *Revue de l'Agriculture,* 36(2), 1983.

Dicloran

FDA, *Surveillance Index,* October 6, 1980.

G. Melkebeke, *et al.,* "Effects of Some Culinary Treatments on Residue Contents of Spinach", (abstract), *Revue de l'Agriculture,* 36(2), 1983.

K. Noren, "Effects of Preparation and Processing on the Concentration of Pesticides in Potatoes, Carrots, and Lentils", (abstract), *Var Foeda,* 27(8/9), 1975.

Dieldrin

EPA, "Aldrin and Dieldrin: Proposed Revocation of Tolerances", 50 Federal Register 10080, March 13, 1985.

S.S. Misra, Lakshman Lal and M.D. Awasthi, "Persistence of Aldrin and Dieldrin Residues in Potatoes", *Journal of Food Science and Technology,* 19:11–19, 1982.

Dimethoate

R.F. Albach and B.J. Lime, "Pesticide Residue Reduction by the Process of Preparing Whole Orange Puree", *Journal of Agricultural and Food Chemistry,* 24:1217–1220, 1976.

E.A. Antonovich and M.S. Vekshtein, "Effect of Various Types of Food Processing on Content of Organophosphorus Pesticide Residues", (abstract), *Voprosy Pitaniya,* 6, 1975.

M. Colakoglu and Y. Hisil, "Removal of Dimethoate and Chlorobenzilate Residues during the Processing of the Apple Juice", (abstract), *Proceedings of the 6th International Congress of Food Science and Technology,* 1, 1983.

EPA, *Dimethoate Registration Standard,* March 1983.

FDA, *Surveillance Index,* revised January 15, 1980.

G. Melkebeke, *et al.,* "Effects of Some Culinary Treatments on Residue Contents of Spinach", (abstract), *Revue de l'Agriculture,* 36(2), 1983.

C. Russo, *et al.,* "Decay of Phosphorylated Insecticides on Sanguinello Moscato Oranges", (abstract), *Essenze Derivati Agrumari,* 53(1), 1983.

Diphenylamine

FDA, *Surveillance Index,* September 16, 1983.

Endosulfan

EPA, *Endosulfan Registration Standard,* April 1982.

V.S. Kavadia and B.L. Pareek, "Residues of Phorate, Carbaryl, and Endosulfan in Peas (*Pisum sativum*)", *Journal of Food Science and Technology,* 18:149–151, 1981.

G. Melkebeke, *et al.,* "Effects of Some Culinary Treatments on Residue Contents of Spinach", (abstract), *Revue de l'Agriculture,* 36(2), 1983.

Ethion

R.F. Albach and B.J. Lime, "Pesticide Residue Reduction by the Process of Preparing Whole Orange Puree", *Journal of Agricultural and Food Chemistry,* 24:1217–1220, 1976.

Fenvalerate

FDA, *Surveillance Index,* January 9, 1981.

Iprodione

FDA, *Surveillance Index,* Supplement No. 10, March 6, 1985.

Lindane

FDA, *Surveillance Index,* November 16, 1979.

S.M. Waliszewski and G.A. Szymczynski, "Bioisomerization of Lindane in Field Conditions", (abstract), *Proceedings of the 6th International Congress of Food Science and Technology,* 1, 1983.

Malathion

R.F. Albach and B.J. Lime, "Pesticide Residue Reduction by the Process of Preparing Whole Orange Puree", *Journal of Agricultural and Food Chemistry,* 24:1217–1220, 1976.

E.A. Antonovich and M. S. Vekshtein, "Effect of Various Types of Food Processing on Content of Organophosphorus Pesticide Residues", (abstract), *Voprosy Pitaniya,* 6, 1975.

G.E. Carman, *et al.,* "Residues of Malathion and Methidathion on and in Fruit after Dilute and Low-volume Spraying of Orange Trees", (abstract), *Bulletin of Environmental Contamination and Toxicology,* 27(6), 1981.

E.R. Elkins, *et al.,* "Removal of DDT, Malathion, and Carbaryl from Green Beans by Commercial and Home Preparative Procedures", *Journal of Agricultural and Food Chemistry,* 16:962–966, 1968.

R.P. Farrow, *et al.,* "Removal of DDT, Malathion, and Carbaryl from Tomatoes by Commercial and Home Preparative Methods", *Journal of Agricultural and Food Chemistry,* 16:65–71, 1968.

G. Melkebeke, *et al.,* "Effects of Some Culinary Treatments on Residue Contents of Spinach", (abstract), *Revue de l'Agriculture,* 36(2), 1983.

G. McDonald, G.A. Buchanan and G.R. Griffiths, "Insecticide Application and Degradation in Sultana Grapes Grown for Drying", *Pesticide Science,* 14:528–536, 1983.

A.R. Shim, E.H. Choi, and S.R. Lee, "Removal of Malathion Residues from Fruits and Vegetables by Washing Processes", (abstract), *Korean Journal of Food Science and Technology,* 16(4), 1984.

Methamidophos

FDA, *Surveillance Index,* May 16, 1980.

Technical Assessment Systems, Inc., *Pesticides in Our Food: Facts, Issues, Debates, and Perceptions,* May 18, 1987.

Methidathion

G.E. Carman, *et al.,* "Residues of Malathion and Methidathion on and in Fruit after Dilute and Low-volume Spraying of Orange Trees", (abstract), *Bulletin of Environmental Contamination and Toxicology,* 27(6), 1981.

EPA, *Methidathion Registration Standard,* January 13, 1983.

FDA, *Surveillance Index,* May 15, 1980.

C. Russo, *et al.,* "Decay of Phosphorylated Insecticides on Sanguinello Moscato Oranges", (abstract), *Essenze Derivati Agrumari,* 53(1), 1983.

Methomyl

EPA, *Methomyl Registration Standard,* October 1981.

FDA, *Surveillance Index,* April 11, 1980.

A.S. Mesallam and Y.G. Moharram, "Removal of Lannate Insecticide from Tomatoes During Processing", (abstract), *Alexandria Journal of Agricultural Research,* 28(3), 1980.

Methyl Parathion

C. Russo, *et al.,* "Decay of Phosphorylated Insecticides on Sanguinello Moscato Oranges", (abstract), *Essenze Derivati Agrumari,* 53(1), 1983.

C. Russo, *et al.,* "Pesticide Residues in Citrus Fruits. III. Persistence of Methyl-Parathion in Microencapsulated Formulations", (abstract), *Industrie Alimentari,* 23(218), 1984.

Mevinphos

FDA, *Surveillance Index,* August 28, 1981.

Parathion

R.F. Albach and B.J. Lime, "Pesticide Residue Reduction by the Process of Preparing Whole Orange Puree", *Journal of Agricultural and Food Chemistry,* 24:1217–1220, 1976.

A.A. Banna and N.S. Kawar, "Behavior of Parathion in Apple Juice Processed into Cider and Vinegar", *Journal of Environmental Science and Health,* B17:505–514, 1982.

R.P. Farrow, *et al.,* "Effect of Commercial and Home Preparative Procedures on Parathion and Carbaryl Residues in Broccoli", *Journal of Agricultural and Food Chemistry,* 17:75–79, 1969.

F.C. Lamb, *et al.,* "Removal of DDT, Parathion, and Carbaryl from Spinach by Commercial and Home Preparative Methods", *Journal of Agricultural and Food Chemistry,* 16:967–973, 1968.

G. Melkebeke, *et al.,* "Effects of Some Culinary Treatments on Residue Contents of Spinach", (abstract), *Revue de l'Agriculture,* 36(2), 1983.

C. Russo, *et al.,* "Decay of Phosphorylated Insecticides on Sanguinello Moscato Oranges", (abstract), *Essenze Derivati Agrumari,* 53(1), 1983.

Permethrin

FDA, *Surveillance Index,* February 24, 1981.

National Academy of Sciences, *Regulating Pesticides in Food: The Delaney Paradox,* 1987.

M. Uno, *et al.,* "Removal of Pyrethroid Insecticides from Agricultural Products by Washing and Boiling", (abstract), *Journal of the Food Hygienic Society of Japan [Shokuhin Eiseigaku Zasshi],* 25(3), 1984.

Phosmet

FDA, *Surveillance Index,* October 5, 1981.

A.S. Sedykh and G.M. Abelentseva, "Removal of Pesticide Residue from Fruit Intended for Canning", (abstract), *Khimiya v Sel'skom Khozyaistve,* 9(3), 1971.

Sulfallate

EPA, "2-Chloroallyldiethyldithiocarbamate: Proposed Tolerance", 46 Federal Register 27973, May 22, 1981.

FDA, *Surveillance Index,* October 21, 1985.

Thiabendazole

FDA, *Surveillance Index,* June 11, 1980.

A. Ibe, *et al.,* "Studies on Fungicides in Citrus Fruits. II. Permeability and Removal of Diphenyl, O-Phenylphenol and Thiabendazole", (abstract), *Annual Report of Tokyo Metropolitan Research Laboratory of Public Health,* 33, 1982.

K. Nakazawa, *et al.,* "Studies on Fungicides in Citrus Fruits. III. The Effect of Cooking on the Movement of Fungicides", (abstract), *Annual Report of Tokyo Metropolitan Research Laboratory of Public Health,* 33, 1982.

K. Yasude, *et al.,* "Studies on Fungicides in Citrus Fruits. I. Market Investigation of Citrus Fruits", (abstract), *Annual Report of Tokyo Metropolitan Research Laboratory of Public Health,* 33, 1982.

Trifluralin

EPA, *Trifluralin Position Document 4,* July 1982.

EPA, *Trifluralin Registration Standard,* August 1986.

FDA, *Surveillance Index,* June 2, 1980.

Vinclozolin

FDA, *Surveillance Index,* Supplement No. 10, April 8, 1985.

M. Meloni, *et al.*, "Residues of Fungicides on Greenhouse Lettuce", *Journal of Agricultural and Food Chemistry*, 32:183–185, 1984.

Sources on information contained in commodity pages

The references used for the text associated with the individual commodities are presented below.

Apples

NRDC, "Daminozide Information Package", June 2, 1987.

"UDMH Found in Most Processed Products Sampled, FDA tells EPA", *Pesticide & Toxic Chemical News*, p. 19, December 24, 1986.

100th Congress, House Committee on Energy and Commerce, Subcommittee on Oversight and Investigations, *Hearing on Pesticide Residues in Food—April 30, 1987,* Data on Selected U.S. Food Imports, prepared by the Congressional Research Service, April 23, 1987.

Leung Cheng, EPA, Memorandum to Walter Waldrop, EPA, "Daminozide Special Review: Phase III Market Basket Survey", May 18, 1987.

Brief of Petitioners, *Nader v. EPA,* No. 87–7103 (9th Circuit filed June 18, 1987).

Bananas

100th Congress, House Committee on Energy and Commerce, Subcommittee on Oversight and Investigations, *Hearing on Pesticide Residues in Food—April 30, 1987,* Statement of J. Dexter Peach, U.S. General Accounting Office, "Federal Regulation of Pesticide Residues in Food."

GAO, *Better Sampling and Enforcement Needed on Imported Food,* September 1986.

Bell peppers

100th Congress, House Committee on Energy and Commerce, Subcommittee on Oversight and Investigations, *Hearing on Pesticide Residues in Food—April 30, 1987,* Statement of J. Dexter Peach, U.S. General Accounting Office, "Federal Regulation of Pesticide Residues in Food."

GAO, *Better Sampling and Enforcement Needed on Imported Food,* September 1986.

Broccoli

Perry Adkisson, *et al.,* "Controlling Cotton's Insect Pests: A New System", *Science,* April 2, 1982.

William Barrett, *et al.,* "Minimizing Pear Control Costs Through Integrated Pest Management", *California Agriculture,* 32:12–13, February 1978.

Dale Botrell, *Integrated Pest Management,* Council on Environmental Quality, 1979.

"Connecticut: Pest Management with IPM", *American Vegetable Grower,* p. 46, April 1983.

R.E. Frisbie and P.L. Adkisson, "IPM: Definitions and Current Status in U.S. Agriculture", in Marjorie A. Hoy and Donald C. Herzog, eds., *Biological Control in Agricultural IPM Systems,* Academic Press, 1985.

United States Congress, Office of Technology Assessment, *Pest Management Strategies in Crop Protection,* p. 6, 1979.

Cabbage

Michael Dover and Brian Croft, *Getting Tough: Public Policy and the Management of Pesticide Resistance,* World Resources Institute, November 1984.

National Academy of Sciences, *Pesticide Resistance,* 1986.

Cantaloupes

100th Congress, House Committee on Energy and Commerce, Subcommittee on Oversight and Investigations, *Hearing on Pesticide Residues in Food—April 30, 1987,* 1987 Correspondence between Congressman Ron Wyden and FDA officials about pesticide violations at West Coast ports.

100th Congress, House Committee on Energy and Commerce, Subcommittee on Oversight and Investigations, *Hearing on Pesticide Residues in Food—April 30, 1987,* Data on Selected U.S. Food Imports, prepared by the Congressional Research Service, April 23, 1987.

Carrots

CDFA, "Notice of Initial Decisions Concerning Reevaluaton of Pesticide Products—Endosulfan", October 21, 1985.

EPA, "Diazinon: Intent to Cancel Registrations and Conclusion of Special Review", 51 Federal Register 35034, October 1, 1986.

Meeting with John Moore, Assistant Administrator for Pesticides and Toxic Substances, EPA, October 19, 1987.

James Serfis, *et al.,* Center for Environmental Education, "The Environmental Protection Agency's Implementation of the Endangered Species Act with Respect to Pesticide Registration", produced for the President's Council on Environmental Quality and the Environmental Protection Agency, July 1986.

Larry Turner, Environmental Effects Branch, EPA, Phone Conversation with Karen Snyder, NRDC, September 4, 1987.

Cauliflower

EPA, "Inert Ingredients in Pesticide Products: Policy Statement", 52 Federal Register 13305, April 22, 1987.

EPA, "Methylene Chloride: Proposed Ban on Use in Aerosol Cosmetic Products", 50 Federal Register 51551, December 18, 1985.

Duncan Saunders, *et al.,* "Outbreak of Omite-CR Induced Dermatitis Among Orange Pickers in Tulane County, California", *Journal of Occupational Medicine,* May 1987.

Celery

Food and Agriculture Organization of the United Nations, *Pesticide Residues in Food—1986: Report of the Joint Meeting of the FAO Panel of Experts on Pesticide Residues in Food and the Environment and the WHO Expert Group on Pesticide Residues,* FAO Plant Production and Protection Paper No. 78, 1986.

Cherries

Robert van den Bosch, *et al., Investigation of the Effects of Food Standards on Pesticide Use,* 1976.
John Walsh, "Cosmetic Standards: Are Pesticides Overused for Appearance's Sake?", *Science,* August 27, 1976.

Corn

EPA, "Alachlor: Notice of Preliminary Determination to Cancel Registrations and Availability of Technical Support Document", October 8, 1986.

Cucumbers

100th Congress, House Committee on Energy and Commerce, Subcommittee on Oversight and Investigations, *Hearing on Pesticide Residues in Food—April 30, 1987,* 1987 Correspondence between Congressman Ron Wyden and FDA officials about pesticide violations at West Coast ports.
100th Congress, House Committee on Energy and Commerce, Subcommittee on Oversight and Investigations, *Hearing on Pesticide Residues in Food—April 30, 1987,* Statement of J. Dexter Peach, U.S. General Accounting Office, "Federal Regulation of Pesticide Residues in Food."
Dynamac Corporation, "The Effects of Production Practices in Eleven Selected Crops on the Potential Exposure of Field Workers to Pesticides", Contract No. 68-01-6072, submitted to EPA on March 31, 1984.
GAO, *Better Sampling and Enforcement Needed on Imported Food,* September 1986.

Grapefruit

CDFA, "Multi-Residue Pesticide Screens", April 24, 1986.
FDA, "Pestrak", May 6, 1986.
Mike McDavit, EPA, Phone Conversation with Karen Snyder, NRDC, September 2, 1987.
NRDC, "EDB Fact Sheet", 1983.
Pesticide Action Network, "The 'Dirty Dozen' Information Packet", Pesticide Education and Action Project, San Francisco, California, 1985.

Grapes

100th Congress, House Committee on Energy and Commerce, Subcommittee on Oversight and Investigations, *Hearing on Pesticide Residues in Food—April 30, 1987,* Data on Selected U.S. Food Imports, prepared by the Congressional Research Service, April 23, 1987.

Green beans

100th Congress, House Committee on Energy and Commerce, Subcommittee on Oversight and Investigations, *Hearing on Pesticide Residues in Food—April 30, 1987,* 1987 Correspondence between Congressman Ron Wyden and FDA officials about pesticide violations at West Coast ports.

GAO, *Better Sampling and Enforcement Needed on Imported Food,* September 1986.

Lettuce

100th Congress, House Committee on Energy and Commerce, Subcommittee on Oversight and Investigations, *Hearing on Pesticide Residues in Food—April 30, 1987,* Statement of J. Dexter Peach, U.S. General Accounting Office, "Federal Regulation of Pesticide Residues in Food."

EPA, "EBDCs: Determination Concluding the Presumption Against Registration", 47 Federal Regulation 47669, October 27, 1982.

FDA, *Surveillance Index,* December 19, 1979.

National Academy of Sciences, *Regulating Pesticides in Food: The Delaney Paradox,* May 1987.

EPA, "EBDCs Pesticides; Initiation of Special Review", 52 Federal Register 27172, July 10, 1987.

Onions

100th Congress, House Committee on Energy and Commerce, Subcommittee on Oversight and Investigations, *Hearing on Pesticide Residues in Food—April 30, 1987,* Data on Selected U.S. Food Imports, prepared by the Congressional Research Service, April 23, 1987.

GAO, *Better Sampling and Enforcement Needed on Imported Food,* September 1986.

Oranges

100th Congress, House Committee on Energy and Commerce, Subcommittee on Oversight and Investigations, *Hearing on Pesticide Residues in Food—April 30, 1987,* Data on Selected U.S. Food Imports, prepared by the Congressional Research Service, April 23, 1987.

Peaches

National Academy of Sciences, *Regulating Pesticides in Food: The Delaney Paradox,* May 1987.

Richard Wiles, National Academy of Sciences, Board on Agriculture, Phone Conversation with Karen Snyder, NRDC, August 24, 1987.

GAO, *Better Sampling and Enforcement Needed on Imported Food,* September 1986.

EPA, *Benomyl Draft Registration Standard,* May 1986.

Pears

Julio Calderon, CDFA, Phone Conversation with Karen Snyder, NRDC, July 2, 1987.

FDA, *Surveillance Index,* January 17, 1980.

National Academy of Sciences, *Regulating Pesticides in Food: The Delaney Paradox,* May 1987.

EPA, *Amitraz Draft Registration Standard,* 1986.

EPA, "Cyhexatin Fact Sheet", September 1987.

CDFA, "CDFA Suspends Registration of Pesticide Plictran", Press Release No. 87–104, June 24, 1987.

Potatoes

EPA, "Dinoseb: Decision and Emergency Order Suspending the Registrations of All Products", 51 Federal Register 36634, October 14, 1986.

Marion Moses, Medical Director of the National Farmworker Health and Safety Group, "Address to the Maryland State Legislature", February 26, 1986.

Robert Wasserstrom and Richard Wiles, *Field Duty: U.S. Farmworkers and Pesticide Safety,* World Resources Institute, July 1985.

Spinach

100th Congress, Senate Committee on Agriculture, *Nutrition and Forestry Hearing on National Academy of Sciences Report—May 20, 1987,* Testimony of Lawrie Mott, NRDC.

National Academy of Sciences, *Regulating Pesticides in Food: The Delaney Paradox,* May 1987.

Strawberries

GAO, *Better Sampling and Enforcement Needed on Imported Food,* September 1986.

Shelley Hearne, *Harvest of Unknowns: Pesticide Contamination in Imported Foods,* NRDC, 1984.

Sweet potatoes

Bryan Bashin, "The Freshness Illusion", *Harrowsmith,* January/February 1987.

NCAMP, "Fungicides Used in Produce Waxes", *Pesticides and You,* June 1987.

Vic Amar, Memorandum to Lawrie Mott, "FFDCA Requirements for Wax and Post-Harvest Pesticide Labeling of Food", July 2, 1987.

Tomatoes

Statement of John A. Moore, Assistant Administrator for Pesticides and Toxic Substances, EPA, before the Committee on Agriculture, Nutrition and Forestry, U.S. Senate, May 20, 1987.

USDA, *Handbook of Agricultural Statistics,* 1983.

GAO, *Better Sampling and Enforcement Needed on Imported Food,* September 1986.

Watermelon

Ken Kizer, DOHS, Memorandum to Clare Berryhill, CDFA, "Request for Reevaluation of Aldicarb (Temik)", February 3, 1986.

Index

Ethanox
  on grapefruit, 80–81
  on onions, 96–97
  on oranges, 100–101
  on pears, 108–109
Ethiol
  on grapefruit, 80–81
  on onions, 96–97
  on oranges, 100–101
  on pears, 108–109
Ethion, 19
  on grapefruit, 13, 80–81
  on onions, 14, 96–97
  on oranges, 14, 100–101
  on pears, 14, 108–109
ETU (ethylenethiourea)
  detection of, 138
  health effects of, 94

F
Farm workers
  effects of dinoseb on, 114
  effects of pesticides on, 7, 110
Federal Food, Drug and Cosmetic
    Act (FFDCA), 126, 135
Federal Insecticide and Rodenticide
    Act (FIFRA), 135
Fenvalerate, 19
  on cabbage, 12, 48–49
Fish, effect of DDT on, 58
Folidol M, 120–121
Folpet, 17
Food
  additives, 11, 136–137
  analysis of, 6–7, 90
  cosmetic appearance of 4, 5, 25,
    70, 126
  imported. *See* Imported food
  labeling, 4
  methods of decreasing pesticides
    in, 22, 24–27
  organic. *See* Organic food
  pesticides in, 1–3, 6–7, 12–15, 17–20,
    21, 22, 24–25. *See also* Pesticides
  processed. *See* Processed foods
  waxed, 30, 126
Food and Drug Administration
    (FDA)
  consumer lobbying of, 26–27

monitoring of imported foods
    by, 17, 20, 22, 90, 138
  monitoring of pesticides by, 4,
    6–7, 9–10, 16–17, 135–138
Formaldehyde, 62
Fungicides, 5, 7
  as wax additives, 126

G
Gamma BHC, 72–73
Grapefruit, pesticide residues in,
    13, 21, 23, 79–81
Grapefruits, 126
Grapes
  EDBCs on, 94
  pesticide residues in, 13, 21, 23
  pesticide residues on, 83–86
Green beans
  dinoseb on, 114
  pesticide residues in, 13, 21, 23
  pesticide residues on, 87–90
Guthion
  on apples, 32–33
  on pears, 108–109

H
HCH
  on cabbage, 48–49
  on sweet potatoes, 124–125
Heinz Company, H. J., 4
Heptachlor
  ban of, 58
  dairy products and, 2
  in humans, 6
Herbicides, 5, 7
Hexachlor
  on cabbage, 48–49
  on sweet potatoes, 124–125
Hexachlorobenzene (HCB), 118

I
Imazalil, as wax additive, 126
Imidan
  on apples, 32–33
  on pears, 108–109
  on sweet potatoes, 124–125
Imported food, 122
  analysis of, 17, 20, 22, 23
  apples as, 34